Endorsements

This devotional book is very inspiring and full of spiritual messages. You will be very blessed by Barb's writings, God has given Bard a heart for writing and has blessed her work. I believe you too will be blessed by this book and I know you will enjoy reading it.

Roger Wilson
National Evangelist
Christian Motorcyclist Association

It is a pleasure for me to endorse Barbara Ann Derksen's new devotional book! As her pastor for the past 11 1/2 years, I have enjoyed watching Barbara grow in the Word of God along with her husband Henry/H.C. Together they have developed a genuine passion for sharing Christ with others, and the Lord has opened many doors of fruitful ministry for them both. Barbara's writing has helped many folks understand what it means to trust in Jesus Christ in a personal way. She has a strong grasp of her true identity as a daughter of God and in this book she creatively illustrates these important truths for others to grow in their spiritual journeys alongside of her. My prayer is that each reader will gain new insight into what it means to be God's adopted child... accepted, secure, significant, and free... through faith in God's one and only Son, our Lord Jesus Christ. To Him be glory forever!

Rev. Doug Corlew

Senior Pastor, Summit Evangelical Free Church, Alta Iowa

1SBN # 978-1-60458-282-6

contact information for
Barbara Ann Derksen
barbd@ncn.net or

barb@barbaraannderksen.com

Two Up

Riding with the LORD

Contemplations from the author

I've thought long about some of the freedom's I've experienced since becoming a Christian. During the early years, I've not seen a lot of respect for women so I've loved studying the scriptures which have women scattered throughout, some in very important roles. During a time in our history and in the Middle East no less, where women today are still considered chattel in a lot of countries, Jesus befriended women, listed them in His genealogy, imparted great news to them, and listened to them.

Mary and Martha were counted as His best friends along with Lazarus, their brother. In Matthew 1:3-6, 5 women – Tamar, Rahab, Ruth, Bathsheba, and Mary are all given credit for their place in the lineage of Christ. When Jesus wanted to let His disciples know that He had risen from the grave, the news was given to women, "Mary Magdalene and the other Mary" according to Matthew 28:1
While He walked the earth, Jesus

talked to a Samaritan woman at the well, raised a widow's son from the dead, and in Luke 8:1-3, the Bible tells of a group of women who traveled with Jesus. The names of three are mentioned but Dr. Luke says there were many others. Remember women during that time were not even allowed an education.

In Judges, chapter 4, God chose a woman by the name of Deborah to lead the Israelites. Deborah was a judge, settling disputes between the people of Israel. Father along in the book of Judges, Jael, wife of Heber, rescued the nation of Israel from a man who was their enemy. In 2 Samuel, the words of a wise woman saves a city and we all know how Esther became Queen for such a time as this and saved the entire nation of Israel from genocide.
Women had important roles in the early church. Two of them, Phoebe and Priscilla were mentioned in the book of Romans, chapter 16. Before that, the book of Proverbs, chapter 31 talks about a woman who does it all; she's a

stay-at-home mom who runs a business and is a loyal wife. There are many other accounts of the importance of women in the Old and New Testaments..

The United States and Canada were founded on the principles outlined in the Bible. Today women have accomplished great things; they raise the next generation who will run our country, run Fortune 500 companies, are doctors, lawyers, financial experts, legislators and a few of them occupy some of the most important seats in our government. Christianity frees women to become who God intends us to be. I believe that if Jesus were with us physically today, he'd be riding a Harley and encouraging women to accomplish their dreams and reach for their goals, no matter how lofty they sometimes appear to be.

I hope the following devotions will touch your heart, whether you are male or female, to see women as important in the scheme of things, and to value their unique gifts from God the Father.

Before we BEGIN

It is God's will that you should be sanctified... 1Thess. 4:3

Sanctified, sanctification – that's a big word. For many, it's hard to understand and yet so important for us to know since it is God's will for us. Sanctification, the move toward Holiness or Christ-likeness, is a process, something that begins when we become a new person in Jesus Christ but something that doesn't occur overnight.

Let me explain. Jodie just gave birth to her first child, a sweet little girl complete with blonde fuzz covering her head. Her innocent expression hid the independent rebellious streak that would one day erupt when her parents least expected it. Was Jodie a mother? She was as far as birthing a child but her journey toward motherhood had just begun.

Over the years, she learned from friends, family members, and books, as well as from The Book – the Bible, how to be the mother that God intended her to be. Did it happen overnight? Not so. In fact, if you asked Jodie today, as a grandmother, she would say she's still learning to parent.

It's the same with sanctification. It's a process. Our walk with the Lord as we study His Word and get to know Him and His will for our lives, takes all the years He gives us in our earthly suits. He allows trials, temptations, events, times of joy and times of sorrow, to refine us into the Christ-like child that He sent His Son to die for. He knows what's in our hearts and He knows just what we need to become sanctified.

What's our part? Study, prayer, and confession. Immediate and consistent confession is so important to our journey for sanctification as the Holy Spirit convicts us of the sin in our lives, the garbage that we hold onto that gives Satan a foothold. God has already forgiven us but we need to acknowledge it in order for forgiveness to heal us from the inside out. We need to pray in the Spirit, asking God a question and then listening for the answer. As we seek God, listen to His answers and the Holy Spirit's promptings, we move closer toward being the Holy person that was created in the image of our Holy God.

Dear Lord, Search me and tell me what unclean thing is within me. Father I acknowledge that I have sinned against You. My desire is to be sanctified now and forevermore. AMEN.

As a Child of God, His Holy Vessel

You are ACCEPTED

Yet to all who received Him, to those who believed in His name, He gave the right to become children of God. John 1:12

Accepted as God's Child

Jenny looked at her birth certificate. For some reason, her father's name was not on it. She decided to ask her mother about it.

For three days, Jenny's mom avoided the conversation but then one morning, she sat down at the kitchen table just as Jenny was about to leave for work. "Your father and I were never married. He was just a date, someone I hardly knew. He got drunk and... I never saw him again." Jenny's mom hung her head. A lone tear trickled down her cheek. "Nine months later you were born."

Jenny's insides felt as if she were on the downward ride on a rollercoaster. She searched her mother's face looking for some sign that she'd heard wrong but her mom's expression said it all. *My mom was raped, Women who are raped today, are pressured to abort their babies.*

Before Jenny could say anything, her mother stood. She wrapped her arms around her only daughter and said, "You were a gift to me from God Himself. I have loved you since the moment I saw you. When I met your father, he fell in love with the two of us. When we married, he adopted you right away."

Being adopted, for Jenny, meant she had a family. She had a father who loved her and two younger brothers who teased relentlessly but were fun to be around anyway. The fact that her father had adopted her as a baby never made her relationship with him any different than the one he had with her brothers. Jenny was taken care of as if she had been born to her dad.

If you have asked Jesus to be the center of your life, you have the privilege of being adopted by the King of Kings and Lord of Lords. You have a Father who loves you, who cares about your deepest desires and who always has time to listen when you talk to Him. You can call Him "Abba" just as if He were your very own daddy.

Hold your head up this day. No matter what your circumstances

NOTES

are, you have a Father who loves you. Under difficult circumstances, or when you are challenged to step out of your comfort zone, He walks beside you and gives you the power to overcome whatever tries to defeat you or mess you up.

If you have never asked Jesus to be the center of your life, you have the opportunity to receive Him now. Pray this simple prayer acknowledging your need for a Savior, and your need for a Father who will love you unconditionally.

Father God, thank you for loving me. I am so sorry I have acted independently from you. Please come into my life and make me your child. Adopt me into your family, Lord. AMEN..

NOTES

I no longer call you servants, because a servant does not know His master's business. Instead, I have called you friends, for everything that I learned from my father I have made known to you.

John 15:15

Accepted as Christ's Friend

Wendy dipped her hands into the detergent as she scrubbed the stains on the clothing in front of her. Her knuckles hurt from rubbing so hard but she hummed a lively tune anyway. Wendy loved her job as housekeeper for Marian Mitchell. Marion never treated her like a servant but more as if she were a treasured friend.

Jesus treats us the same way. He is King of Kings and Lord of Lords. He deserves to see us bow down before Him in submission but instead He calls us friend. He could have

created us with loyalty to Him built in but instead He gave us free will so that when we seek Him, it will be because we want to. He only requests a genuine love, one that comes from our heart. He asks that anything we do for Him is because we love Him, not because we feel we have to obey Him.
Wendy loved the Lord. She was working as a housekeeper for Marian but also working for the Lord. Because she loved Him, she did her work to the best of her ability without complaining. Marian valued her loyalty and counted it a privilege to call Wendy her friend. Marian treated her as equal just as Christ treats us as brothers and sisters.

Lord, thank you for calling me to be a friend and not a servant. Thanks you for treating me as your equal when I know that is not the case. I love you Lord. AMEN..
If you meant these words in your heart, Christ accepts you as if you had always been part of His family. He now calls you brother or sister affording you the privilege of access to the Father through Him.

Therefore since we are all justified through faith, we have peace with God through our Lord Jesus Christ. Roman 5:1

NOTES

Justified through Faith

Diane walked through the doorway. Her tiny apartment seemed huge compared to the place where she'd spent the last five years. There was no clanging of iron bars, no shouting, no cursing, and above all, no one telling her when to go to bed and when to get up each morning. Peace.

Diane also had peace in her heart. There was no one coming after her to put her behind bars. She'd paid her debt to society. She'd paid the price she owed the state for her bad choices.

Jesus was the one who paid the price owed to God for our bad choices. Because of Him, we don't have to wonder if someday God will reign down punishment on our heads. He sent His Son to hang on a cross, bruised and battered for our sins. We can enjoy peace with Almighty God, our just and faithful Creator because of Christ. God can hear us, see us, and watch over us with nothing separating us from His love for us...thanks to Jesus we are accepted into His kingdom as His children.

Father, I can never pay the price, the debt, I owe for ignoring You most of my life. I've treated others badly and wanted my own selfish way. Thank you for providing a way for me to find peace with you…a way to feel forgiven even when I don't deserve it. AMEN.

NOTES

But he who unites himself with the Lord is one with Him in spirit.
1Cor.6:17

United with the Lord

Mary sat quietly reading a book. She was absorbed with the details of the mystery that the characters were enacting so didn't respond when her husband John shouted loudly toward the television screen. He usually got excited when he watched his favorite sports program.

Looking up, Mary decided to go to the fridge. She pulled a cold pop off the shelf, poured it into a glass and walked back into the family room. John smiled at her as she approached and handed him the drink.

"How did you know I wanted something to drink?"

"I just knew." She smiled and returned to her seat and the mystery she was dying to finish. John shook his head and resumed watching TV.

Mary and John could sometimes sense what each other thought or wanted without any words spoken between them. Have you ever noticed the same thing between couples who have a committed relationship and have been married for a long time?

God's Holy Spirit becomes united with ours when we accept Jesus as Lord of our life. God's Spirit communes with us and goes wherever we go to instill in us God's sense of right and wrong. His Spirit is our comforter when we are distressed over something.

Being united with Christ, means sharing a common Spirit as His Spirit joins ours. As we study God's word, spend time with Him daily, our thoughts become more in tune with God's provision for us... His will for our lives through the Holy Spirit.

Father God, thank you for sending Your Spirit to indwell us, to comfort us, and to keep our conscience sharp. Help us not to offend Him by doing things that are wrong. Keep us sharp Lord by allowing Your Spirit to strengthen us against temptation. AMEN.

Do you not know that your body is a temple of the Holy Spirit, who is in you, whom you have received from God? You are not your own; you were bought at a price. Therefore honor God with your body. 1Cor. 6:19-20

NOTES

Accepted by God

When Terry and Janice moved into the trailer park, they were given a set of rules. When they filled out an application, they promised to obey those rules. They were happy to do so.

Rules and standards for living are common everyday occurrences but many people think that there are no rules in regards to their own body. They think they have the right to do whatever they want with it. So drugs, drinking alcohol and sex outside of marriage become a way of life. Eventually their body begins to break down, develop a disease or two and their immune system is taxed

to the limit.
Terry and Janice knew that if there were rules for them to obey, everyone else also had to obey those same rules and all residences would benefit from the lack of loud music, safe streets, and well kept yards.
When we become part of God's family by accepting Jesus as our Lord and Savior, we have an obligation to obey God's rules concerning our bodies, the very bodies Christ died on the cross to redeem. While Christ's death freed us from sin, His Holy Spirit lives in us. We have an obligation not to violate the building He lives in.

Father, show me how to keep my body pure. Help me study Your Word and learn all that You want me to learn about my obligation to live according to Your will. AMEN.

NOTES

Now you are the body of Christ, and each one of you is part of It.
1Cor. 12:27

Accepted as a Member of Christ's Body

Cynthia walked slowly, step by step, down the aisle. Ahead of her, just to the right of the aisle was her soon-to-be husband Paul. Cynthia felt the tears begin as her dreams were about to be realized. She'd grown up as a foster child. No one had ever adopted her so she'd never belonged to a family of her own. Although, the people who were her foster parents were nice, they still were not her parents, her family, especially once she'd turned 18. Then she was on her own.

After today, Cynthia would belong to Paul's family. They would be her in-laws, her family, and they had already shown her the love she'd always dreamed of. Cynthia happily placed her hand in Paul's out-stretched palm and

the ceremony began.
When we belong to Christ, we are a member of His family, a child of God Almighty. We have all the privileges of being part of the family of God but we also have all the responsibilities too, just as Cynthia was responsible to the family she was marrying into.
What a wonderful place to be, a member of God's family. Do you think He expects only perfection? He knows you. He knows you'll mess up from time to time but He welcomes you into His family anyway.

Father God, thank you for allowing me a place in your family. Thank you for treating me as Your child and allowing me to hold my head high as I embrace Your love for me. AMEN.

NOTES

Paul, an apostle of Christ Jesus by the will of God, to the saints in Ephesus, the faithful in Christ Jesus.

Eph 1:1

Accepted as a Saint

Jeremy drove his Fat Boy in riding formation. Behind and ahead of him there were bikes as far as the eye could see and he knew they presented a formidable group of men and women. People stopped to stare. They pointed as the bikers passed, ignoring stop signs and riding through intersections as a unit. Jeremy saw many shake their head.

The group pulled up to a bar, parked their bikes, and walked, swaggering, into the dimly lit interior. They laughed together as if privy to a secret only they knew. The bar's patrons vacated tables to move towards the booths located along the far wall. The bikers took over.

"Hey, girlie. Bring us some beer." The loudest and the fiercest looking leader of the pack, Wolverine, pounded his hand on the table to accent his wishes. He looked at Jeremy. "Drinking tonight, Jer?"

"Sure," Jeremy replied, "just not beer." When the bar maid approached their table, Jeremy asked for a coke in a can. Wolverine laughed derisively. "When're you gonna give up all that religious stuff? You're strong, just like me. You don't need no crutch."

"My faith is not a crutch and you of all people should know that."

"I know, I know. You don't do nothin' you don't believe your God wants you to do but..."

"No buts Wolverine. Either I believe or I don't. You need God too. You just don't know it yet. But if, one of these nights, a car takes you down, where you gonna be? I know that if that happens to me, I'll live the rest of my life with Jesus Christ. If I'm wrong, what have I lost? A hangover? But if you're wrong, you lose any chance at a perfect life for eternity."

"Yeah, yeah. I heard it before." Wolverine edged away from the table and walked over to the jukebox. He pounded his money into the slot and loud raucous music blared. He grabbed the nearest woman and began to gyrate to the beat.

Jeremy was a Christian and wherever he went, he was faithful to his Lord, even when riding with this group of bikers. According to Ephesians 1:1, Paul calls him a saint, one of the faithful in Christ Jesus. You are too, if you practice your walk to pattern your talk as Jeremy did.

NOTES

Lord, strengthen me for the walk you have called me to. Keep me close and allow me to act as your representative in front of whomever you send my way. AMEN..

For through Him we both have access to the Father by one Spirit.
Eph 2:18

Direct Access to God Through the Holy Spirit

Deborah drove the water cart through the campground looking for hand signals that would indicate someone was thirsty. She watched as many waved beer cans in her direction, or used derogatory motions to indicate she was an intruder. Deborah smiled. She proudly carried her faith around her like a cloak, warding off cuss words, crude gestures, and the tiredness that came from a sleepless night.

Just as she was about to leave that section of the rally site, a man raised his head. His sad eyes portrayed an agony inside. From what, Deborah could only guess. He stood slowly. She watched as he raised his hand, but then put it down again. He shook his head. Deborah moved on.

Later that day, she was traveling through that same section, overshadowed by trees. The temperature had risen to an uncomfortable level but she still smiled. The shade under these trees caused the heat index to drop slightly. As she passed the man

NOTES

with the sad eyes, working her way toward the back of this group of tents, she noticed him sitting as before, head bent and a crushed can of beer at his feet.

Deborah turned around and headed back the way she'd come. The man waved and stood. She stopped. He walked slowly toward her and as she poured him a refreshing cup of water, he began to speak.

"Thank you Ma'am, but it's not water I need. My son is leaving this weekend to travel with a rock band. I know you have a connection to God. All you people do. Would you ask God to protect my son?" His eyes looked on her with confidence that she could do as he asked.

"Why don't we pray right now?" Deborah put the cup of water on the side of the cart. As she closed her eyes, she saw him look around to see if anyone was watching. He shrugged and bowed his head.

Non-believers accept that we who are believers have access to God. What a privilege that is. Only a believer can stand before the throne of Grace and know that

Jesus Christ intercedes on our behalf before God the Father. This man knew that members of Deborah's biker group were Christians and that they practiced what they believed. They had access to God but so do you, if Jesus is Lord of your life.

Father God, Thank you for the comfort we have as believers. We know You are listening to us and we know that we can come to You at any time to access your strength and your guidance. AMEN.

And you have been given fullness in Christ, who is the head over every power and authority.
Col 2:10

NOTES

Complete in Christ

Marsha struggled with the task in front of her. She needed to complete this one before she could begin the next. *There is always a next one*, she thought. She had a hard time saying no. Marsha loaded the table with fresh produce for the food bank and then picked up the inventory list, Keeping track of what came in and what was taken by needy people in the community was part of her job as food bank coordinator.

Marsha loved the accolades she received from leaders in the small town she lived in. And yet, she was never satisfied that she'd done enough or that she received enough community awards. She felt a deep emptiness inside. These volunteer projects were supposed to fill that void, guarantee her a place of honor in heaven some

day. Nothing seemed to be good enough, however.
As a Christian, God has come into our lives to fill that empty spot, the void that was created so that only He could fill it. People try all sorts of things, working hard to load that emptiness with good deeds but they leave God entirely out of the picture. It doesn't work.
Our walk with the Lord, our daily time with Him, fills us to continue through the rest of our day. Because we are content, because we feel loved and cherished by God Himself, we seek to volunteer, to do whatever we can for someone else, not so we can earn anything but because of what He has given to us. We want to share His love with others because He gave His love to us when we least deserved it. Our life is full, content, and we have only God to thank for it.

Lord, I do thank You for my life, for the fullness and contentment I feel daily. Thank you for filling me with Your love so I can give it away to others. AMEN.

NOTES

He predestined us to be adopted as His sons through Jesus Christ , in accordance with His pleasure and will

Eph. 1:5

Adopted as God's Child

Betty struggled to open her eyes. She shivered under the thin blanket that covered her as she peeked out of the cardboard box she was lying in. "Another day, scrounging to get enough to eat," she mumbled, with lips thick from an infection that seemed to last a long time. The cuts were healing but her warm forehead told her that her body was harboring some bug or another.

"Hey, kid. Let's go before the thugs wake up. You 'member what happened the last time you slept all day?" Herman shook her box. She'd begun to walk the streets with him, in hopes of some protection.

"Aw right, aw right. I'm comin'." She stretched her tiny arms, rolled over and stood on legs that ached from the cold. She wrapped the blanket around her, over the three sweaters and coat she already wore. She placed one foot in front of the other, hoping she'd not pass out somewhere or get beat up again.

"You need a family," Herman limped beside her. He knew he was an old man. He could die any night now. Betty'd told him she was about ten years old. As far as she could remember anyway. She was a sweet thing, but soon the thugs would do more to her than just beat on her.

"You know my family's gone," she sniffed, swiping her arm across her runny nose. "No one wants me."

"I know where we can get you a family." Herman looked at her with sad eyes. He could get her good food but a family...that was another thing. "Come on. We're goin' to the shelter."

"No Herman. They'll put me in jail. I don't want to go to jail."

"Who told you that? They will find you a home, not jail. I know. I went there once and watched them do that for another little one like you." Herman straightened his back, as much as he could, bent his head and looked her straight in the eye. "You're too young to make it on the streets. Besides, someone out there has the perfect home for you."

Herman and Betty traipsed halfway across the city to the shelter. Within two weeks, Betty had parents who were

NOTES

thrilled to have a ten-year old child to call their own. Their immediate love was unconditional. They clothed her with new jeans, shirts, and a dress or two for good measure. They hugged her as often as she'd let them. Betty was happy for the first time since her parents had abandoned her.

God does that for us. He adopts us into His family, gives us unconditional love, and provides for our needs on a daily basis. We are His children and He is our Father. Imagine. **Children of the King of Kings and Lord of Lords.**

Dear God, Thank you for providing a family for me, for adopting me into Your family. Thank you for loving me unconditionally. I love you Lord. AMEN.

For He has rescued us from the dominion of darkness and brought us into the Kingdom of the Son He loves in whom we have redemption, the forgiveness of sins. Col.1:13-14

Redeemed and Forgiven

Brenda hung her head. "Maybe you don't want me for a room-mate. I had a baby last year and I placed her for adoption." She stepped toward the door.

The woman in front of Brenda shook her head. "I don't care what your morals are. I only want the rent paid on time. Can you do that?" Brenda went on to tell Joyce that she had a full time position with a bank and that meeting her financial obligations would not be a problem. Joyce said the room was hers if she wanted it. Brenda was elated but inside, she continued to feel unworthy of anyone's time and energy. Brenda carried her feelings of inferiority for years. She considered herself blessed when a good man asked her to be his wife but she felt unworthy of him. So before too long she began to look for things that he didn't like about her. Their arguments escalated but her husband never fully understood what the root cause

NOTES

was. Brenda had told him about her former boyfriend's mistreatment of her and the resulting pregnancy. He said he was tired of paying for that man's selfishness, though.

One day, after about 4 years of marriage and many discussions of divorce, Brenda sat down and read a book that outlined God's plan of salvation. She discovered that God, as Jesus Christ, had allowed Himself to be nailed to a cross after suffering horrible torture at the hands of Roman soldiers.

She also discovered that in doing so, He had paid the penalty for her sins, even the one of having a baby before marriage. He loved her so much that He was willing to take her sin into His own body and die, a penalty set out by a just God for her independence from Him. Brenda began to cry.

Her tears were cleansing tears. She realized how loved she was, how forgiven she was, and how much God had done for her in providing a husband who also loved her just as she was. She felt clean inside for the first time in 7 years. "So this is what forgiveness feels like," she spoke out loud to no one in particular. She wanted to phone her husband, to tell him her good news but she didn't. *What if this is not real*, she thought. Brenda phoned two women who attended the church where she and her husband had married. They came for a visit the next day and pointed out all the Bible verses that spoke about her commitment to Jesus and what He had done for her. Brenda was a changed person, inside and out as every day from that time on, she worked hard to show Jesus how grateful she was and to show others how they could feel clean inside and out, like she did. Christians can accept that Jesus paid the penalty for our sins. When God judges the wicked, there will be nothing for Him to judge in our case because He has erased all the wrong's we have committed, thanks to Jesus. You can feel clean on the inside as well as on the outside just like Brenda. Believe that Jesus did what the Bible said He did, accept that you need Him to control your life and pray with me:

Lord, thank you for dying on the cross for me. I don't deserve it but I accept your gift of love. Please walk with me every day and help me lean only on You. AMEN.

As a member of God's family, You are SECURE

Therefore there is now no condemnation for those who are in Christ Jesus because through Christ Jesus the law of the Spirit of Life set me free from the law of sin and death. Romans 8:1-2

Free from Condemnation

Cynthia sat, back straight, on her bunk, the only place for her to sit in her tiny cell. Her face showed little emotion, a trait learned over the last five years as she languished on death row. It wouldn't be long now. She looked at her watch. Just 12 more hours and her life would end. She cringed and then looked toward the guards standing nearby to see if they'd noticed.

Cynthia had been convicted of murdering three people. She was guilty. She knew it and so did the jury who convicted her. But she still hoped that her lawyer would be able to overturn the verdict. She'd changed in this place and she wanted another chance. The law said, "No." At least it had so far. Cynthia looked again at her watch. Another five minutes had passed and still no word from the man who had represented her from the beginning.

NOTES

We are like Cynthia, condemned to death for living life independently of a Holy God. We deserve to die just as God pronounced when Adam and Eve submitted their will to that of Satan in the Garden of Eden. But, we have been redeemed. Jesus Christ died in our place. He walked the last mile, suffered on the cross as if an electric jolt from the electric chair had shot through His body or the gas flowing in air currents through the chamber had cut off His last breath.

Not only did He pay the price demanded from a Holy God, a just God, but He also made a way for us to never be chained to sin again. Each time, when we're tempted to follow someone or something down that wrong path, we can gaze heavenward and know that with His power we can say "NO" and walk in the opposite direction. Once we've bowed to the Father's will for our lives, we can be secure in the knowledge that He pronounced us "NOT GUILTY" and given us the power to escape bondage to sin.

Father God, thank You. Thank You that You sent Your Son to die for my sins. Thank You that I can feel secure in Your love for me and in the knowledge that I don't have to bow to Satan's will any more. AMEN.

And we know that in all things God works for the good of those who love Him, who have been called according to His purpose. Romans 8:28

NOTES

All Works Together for Good

The phone rang. Its shrill jangle echoed through the downstairs as Jennifer ran towards the kitchen. Her hand trembled. She picked up the receiver and placed it next to her ear. "Hello." She ran a hand over her skirt, smoothing wrinkles not there.

"Miss Canton?" The voice seemed kindly but Jennifer had heard about his reputation as a calculating business man.

"Y-yes."

"Miss Canton, I would like you to begin working for me as soon as you can. Could you start tomorrow?" His voice brought relief and the beginning crinkles of a smile to her face.

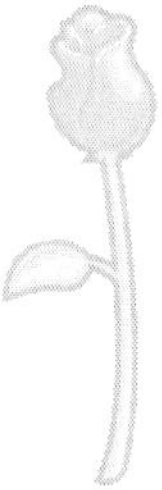

"Yes, yes I can. What time does

the office open?" Jennifer's legs almost buckled. She'd been chosen for the job of a lifetime, one that she'd prayed for and worked hard to earn.

God has chosen us, called us according to His purposes (the job of a lifetime), not ours. Unlike Jennifer's new boss, who called her for what she could do for him, God will work all things out for OUR good when we turn our life over to His purpose. That doesn't mean that bad things won't happen to us. However, God will use even those circumstances for our eventual good and for His glory.

When God calls us, the Holy Spirit convinces and enables us to receive Christ. We learn to trust in God, not life's fading treasures. We begin to see life from God's perspective, loving people as He does and because He does. God's purpose filled life for us is the most meaningful and one that will earn us eternal rewards. Our security is in heaven, not on earth.

Father, thank You for working things out so that no matter what, they end up for my good and for Your glory. Help me trust in you and place my security in heaven, not on things of this world. AMEN.

NOTES

If God is for us, who can be against us? He who did not spare His own son, but gave Him up for us all – how will He not also, along with Him, graciously give us all things? Who will bring any charge against those whom God has chosen? It is God who justifies. Who is he that condemns? Christ Jesus who died – more than that, who was raised to life - is at the right hand of God and is also interceding for us. Romans 8: 31b-34

Free From the Charges Against Me

Jocelyn looked across the courtyard. Her eyes misted as she watched her neighbor hug the little boy. She and her husband had adopted him just four weeks ago. They accepted him into their family as if they'd given birth to him, as if he were their own child. "Well I guess he is now."

Jocelyn walked away from the window and plopped down on her beat-up sofa. *If only*, she thought. *If only I'd been adopted and not had to spend my first 18 years in foster homes. Maybe I would have turned out better.* A tiny tear slid down her cheek. Now it was too late. Now she had a felony record attached to her name.

Jocelyn believed she was not worth anyone's time and attention. She was afraid to venture too far from her apartment in case she was picked up for another offense, maybe one that this time she didn't commit. She felt everyone was out to get her and throw her back into jail. As the week progressed, she began to think about ending her life.

One day, her neighbor knocked on her door. Jocelyn peeked through the front window curtains and saw a plate of cookies in her hands. She slowly opened the door. "Yes, what do you want?" She was almost afraid to ask.

"I've brought you some cookies. I baked them this morning." The woman handed Jocelyn the plate.

Jocelyn's hand shook as she held the plate in front of her. "Why would you do that? Why bring them to me? Doesn't your kid like cookies?" Jocelyn backed up a step or two. She used the door as a shield.

NOTES

"Oh, sure he likes cookies but we have plenty. I just want us to be friends, is all. Could you use another friend?" The woman smiled. Jocelyn believed that since she was a felon, she didn't deserve anything. However, God in His Word, says that since He already gave us His best, His Son to die for us, there is nothing He would not provide for us. Jocelyn accepted Jesus as her Lord and Savior in prison. Now, she was about to experience some of the good things He had in store for her. Her neighbor invited her to church, and her husband offered Jocelyn a job. Soon they were having coffee together all the time.

Jocelyn began to understand how she needed to forgive herself, accept God's love for her and stop feeling guilty and worthless. He had sent His Son to die for her, to pay the price for her sins and she was a new creation. She began to experience security for the first time in her life and she knew that Jesus was her council before God, pleading her case.

Lord God, thank You for interceding, for pleading my case before God the Father. Thank You for providing a way for my salvation and for allowing me to begin eternal life with you, right now here on earth. AMEN.

Who shall separate us from the love of Christ? Shall trouble or hardship or persecution or famine or nakedness or danger or sword?.... For I am convinced that neither death nor life, neither angels nor demons, neither the present nor the future, nor any powers, neither height nor depth, nor anything else in all creation, will be able to separate us from the love of God that is in Christ Jesus our Lord.

Romans 8:35-36; 38-39

NOTES

Cannot be Separated From God's Love

Cheryl wandered along the bank of the river she'd loved since childhood. The soothing sound of water lapping on the shore erased any worry she had... almost. Her husband had lost his job and he'd been accused of em-

bezzling company funds. What were they going to do if he went to jail?

She sat down on a nearby rock and pulled a blade of grass. As she rolled it around in her fingers, some Bible verses came to mind. She knew beyond a shadow of a doubt that God loved her. She also knew that God said in His Word, that nothing could separate her from that love, even her husband going to jail. Cheryl remembered the speaker who'd come to their church just three weeks ago. Did God know that she'd need to hear those words back then? The man was Chinese and he'd been imprisoned for believing in Jesus Christ. He'd spent 20 years in captivity, away from his family and with little food to eat but he'd trusted that His God would bring him through. While in prison, he'd met and married his wife in secret. That tiny woman sat with him on the platform and also told of her time in prison. They knew that God had carried them through this ordeal and were eager to return to their native land to tell others again about Jesus, even if it meant that they would face imprisonment again.

God brought them through. Cheryl stood, dusted her pants off, and began to walk home. Her husband needed her and so did her children. She would support them and lean on God for his protection on a daily basis. He was her

Savior and nothing else mattered. **NOTES**

Father, thank You for Your love no matter what, for not allowing anything to come between Your love and us. Keep us safe and in Your care. AMEN.

Now it is God who makes both us and you stand firm in Christ. He anointed us, set His seal of ownership on us, and put His Spirit in our hearts as a deposit, guaranteeing what is to come.
2 Cor. 1:21-22

Established, Anointed, Sealed by God

Judy picked up the patch and looked at the details. It signified that she belonged to the gang and that nothing could change that. She shivered slightly but knew that Beetle would not let her leave. She sat down in front of the sewing machine and began to permanently attach the patch to the back of her leather vest. The gang owned her as if she was a piece of property and there was nothing she could do about it.

Once we've made the choice to follow Jesus, God seals us with His seal of ownership. We belong to Him and are protected by Him. We are referred to in the Bible as His Holy vessels. We can be proud to call Him Father and Lord. He sends the Holy Spirit who guarantees that we belong to Him and will receive all the benefits of belonging.

Unlike the gang that Judy belongs to, God will not use us

NOTES

or abuse us. He is incapable of doing so. He loves us so much that He wants only what is best for us, for our good. The Holy Spirit, as our comforter, gives us a glimpse of what heaven will be like as we live according to the Holy Scriptures.

Judy had to prove herself in a variety of ways before the gang extended membership to her. God only asks that we tell others about Him. We need to identify with Him and not be ashamed to share the Gospel with a hurting world.

Lord God, I love you and I love that I belong to You, that nothing can change that, not even my sinful self. Holy Spirit, grant me the grace to love others in such a way that I can't help but share the Good News with them. AMEN.

For you died and your life is now hidden with Christ in God.
Col. 3:3

Hidden with Christ in God

Barbara excitedly filled in the Publisher's Clearing House entry form. Maybe one day she would win a million dollars. Just before Easter, later that year, she opened an envelope from another lottery. In it, she read that she'd won $30,000. Barbara was so excited she could hardly wait to tell her boyfriend when he came over after work.

Jerry knocked on the door and Barbara was ready. Before he had a chance to say one word, she blurted, "Guess what? I won. I won. See this letter." She waved the paper in front of him, almost hitting his eye. Jerry backed up and then grabbed the fluttering article.

"Barbara, this is a scam. All they want you to do is send them some money. Honestly, honey, you are so gullible."

"How do you know that? It could be true."

"Why not stick with something you know is true. Remember when you accepted Christ as your personal Savior? That's true. That's not just wishful thinking or something that will go away or is a scam. That's forever true. Nothing and no one

can take that away from you." Jerry was right. The Bible says that your life is hidden – that is protected and safe – with Christ, once you have asked Him to be your Lord and Savior. You don't have to win anything or work hard to earn anything. It's a free gift given to you once and for all time. Your salvation is safe and a sure thing. Gambling is addictive. We are tempted to strive for the unattainable. Why not seek the attainable in Christ Jesus? Why not live with the assurance that our life is secure and safe, protected from the enemy as we resist by putting on the whole armor that the Bible talks about? Seek a Holy God, and all the things that are important in life will be given to you.

Father God. I love You. Help me seek the things from above, the things that really matter in life instead of grasping for what is of no consequence. Remind me often Holy Spirit to put on God's armor so I will be able to resist the evil one. AMEN.

NOTES

He who began a good work in you will carry it on to completion until the day of Christ Jesus.

Phil. 1:6

Confident God will Continue the Work He began in Me

Jeremy lay quietly in his hospital bed...amazed. He'd had a transplant just two days ago and already he was feeling so much better. The doctors had been optimistic but they'd never explained what a difference the new bone marrow could make in such a short time. Jeremy's wife, Carol, sat by his bed.

"Honey, it's almost as if I can feel the new bone marrow coursing through my bones. I feel so much better already."

"I am thankful the doctor suggested this, aren't you?" Carol stood and moved closer to the bed. She sat on the edge. "It's a little like what the pastor said on Sunday at church. Once a person accepts Jesus into their heart, God begins working in us and continues to do so until we enter heaven. Your new bone marrow is continuing to do good work for your body as we sit here."

"Hey, that's a good analogy. God works in us to perfect us, to make us more Christ-like every day, and the bone marrow is working in me

NOTES

to perfect my blood and my body. I still get so tired but not the kind of weary that made me almost wish for the end to come. That was not fun, even though I knew I'd be in heaven if I died." Jeremy laid his head back on the pillow. "I think I'll take a nap. Is that alright?"

Carol smiled. "Rest, husband of mine. I'll finish reading this chapter from the book of John." She knew talking too much still taxed his strength. She watched as he snuggled under the blanket and closed his eyes. He was almost the same man that she'd married, except for his energy level. She walked quietly back to her chair and picked up the Bible she'd been reading before Jeremy had interrupted her.

Carol bowed her head. "Father, thank You for working in my heart to make me the kind of person acceptable to You. Thank you for never giving up on me, even when I question your methods for perfecting me. AMEN."

God, continue to work in my heart. Thank You for seeking my good above my selfish desires.

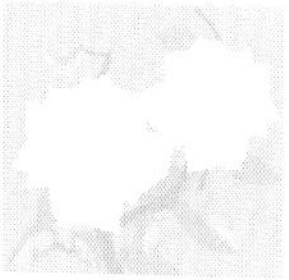

Thank You for being faithful to Your promises. AMEN.

But our citizenship is in heaven. And we eagerly await a Savior from there, the Lord Jesus Christ.
Phil.3:20

NOTES

Citizen of Heaven

Renee spoke French, was a native of France, and loved everything about her country. After moving to the United States, for a time, she continued to speak her native language, cook all her favorite dishes, and speak volumes, to anyone who would listen, about all the good things her country had to offer.

"Renee, why did you move to the States if you love France so much? Maybe you should move back." Jackson was tired of listening to her regale her country when she'd relinquished her citizenship to live in his country.
"Oh but, I don't want to move back, eh. I came...um...because I want to learn English, and because I want to make a better life for me, non. What is so wrong wit that, huh?"

"Then you need to become American. Your citizenship is in this country so it is about this country that you should speak and learn. France was your country but you've chosen to seek what this country has to offer. Now you should promote the States, live like an American, and learn what there is to love about us."

"Oh Oui. I see dat. I agree."

Renee, although she lived in an English speaking country, still spoke French most of the time. She promoted France. It's the same for us if we continue to live as if our citizenship was of this world and not in heaven. Christ paid a price so we could become citizens of heaven one day. We should speak about and promote the things that will bring others into the kingdom that we love.

Lord Jesus, thank You for dying on the cross so I could become a citizen of heaven. Holy Spirit help me think on things of heaven and not lust after things here on earth. AMEN.

NOTES

For God did not give us a spirit of timidity but a spirit of power, of love, and of self -discipline.

2 Tim. 1:7

A Spirit of Power, Love, and Sound Mind

Cindy walked into the rally quaking in her motorcycle boots. Why was she here? She wandered through the line of bikes flanking the entrance and strode over toward some friends. “This is scary,” she whispered.

Her friend, a veteran of this rally, giggled. “You’ll get over it. Once you see all the hurting people here, people who need to know Jesus as Lord and Savior, you’ll forget all about being scared.”
“I don’t know. What if I say the wrong thing? What if one of those mean looking guys over there tries to hit on me. What do I say? How do I handle that without ticking him off?” Cindy felt a lone tear leak from beneath her sunglasses.
“Cindy, don’t you know? God

gives us the spirit of power, love and self-discipline to do and say what He wants us to do and say here. This is His ministry. Do you really think He'd ask people who might mess up His ministry to join Him here? I don't think so."

Cindy thought about what her friend said. Her pastor had preached, a few weeks ago, about how God does not give us fear, the enemy does. Did that mean the enemy didn't want her in this place? And if that was the case, how was God going to use her that would cause Satan to cringe?

She smiled. God had provided her with the necessary tools to minister to bikers...His power, His love, and His self-discipline. WOW. Watch out Satan, here I come.

Dear Lord, remind me often that You are in control. Help me tap into your power, love and self-discipline. Thank You for providing the tools I need to witness for you. AMEN.

Let us then approach the throne of Grace with confidence so that we may receive mercy and find grace to help us in our time of need. Heb. 4:16

NOTES

Grace and Mercy in Time of Need

Cold wind whipped her hair as Jet parked her bike closest to the door of the church. She wanted to be able to make a quick get-away in case they didn't want her in this place. Jet had accepted Christ as her personal Lord and Savior just two weeks ago. She was now taking the next step. Church.

She took two steps toward the door. "Naw, maybe next week." Jet turned, walked the two steps back toward her Shadow, and straddled the black leather seat. This she was comfortable with. She sat awhile and watched.
A young couple walked across the parking lot with three small children behind...like ducks walking after their mother. Jet smirked.

She wanted so much to be like that. They walked confidently. They knew where they were going.

Just as they entered the building, another person caught her attention. This woman was about the age of her grandmother. Although she walked with a cane for support, she too walked with confidence into the building. Jet sighed. "If only..."

"If only what?" The voice spoke behind her. Jet turned. She saw an old man, crippled with age, bent over at the waist but smiling from ear to ear.

"What're you lookin at?" She turned, back straight, and huffed. "I was just sittin here."

"No you weren't." The old man walked slowly to stand beside her. "Little lady, you wanted to come inside. I saw you get off your bike earlier. What is the 'if only' all about?"

"Never mind. I guess. Anyway, I don't fit in." She hung her head and picked at a hole in her jeans.

The man chuckled. Jet glared at him. "How're you goin ta know ifin you don't come in? Come with me, why doncha?"

Jet shrugged her shoulders. She did want to go in. Maybe. She slowly got off the bike, straightened her leather jacket, pulled down the legs on her jeans and walked to stand beside her new friend. "Sure you wanna be seen with me?"

"I'm sure." He placed a hand on her arm and together they walked through the doors.

NOTES

God wants us to approach Him in prayer ...with confidence. We never have to fear or be intimidated by His Majesty. We just have to talk as if He was our best Friend, our Counselor, but with reverence, After all, He is the Almighty King of Kings, our King.

Father, I am confident of Your love for me. I am sure that You are the faithful one in this partnership. Thank You for Your gentleness and kindness. AMEN.

We know that anyone born of God does not continue to sin; the One who was born of God keeps him safe, and the evil one cannot harm him. 1John 5:18

The evil one cannot touch me

Jess stumbled. She raked her arm across the rough brickwork in the process causing scratches to compete for space on her emaciated body. Her vision blurred. Time to rest. She sat down hard on the wet pavement in the alleyway. A box leaned haphazardly near the dumpster. Jess moved toward it, crawling. She rolled inside and fell into a drugged sleep.

The next morning, she woke with a start. She looked around and then remembered her box. It felt as if it was being lifted off the ground. She peeked outside. Two men were carrying her box, with her in it, toward the dumpster.

"Hey, let me out." She coughed.

The men rolled the box, dumped her on the ground and then laughed. "Another dope head." They sneered and then threw the box into the trash. They stalked off, shaking their head in disgust.

Jess scratched her backside, sniffed the cold air into her lungs, and then sauntered toward the park. She needed a fix, bad.

NOTES

The park was a short two blocks from her alleyway. She moved as fast as her thin body could go until she spied just the man she wanted to see. Just as she was about to make contact, another woman walked toward her. Jess didn't recognize her.

"Hey Jess, remember me. I'm Kate."

"Kate? Wow, you look good. What you gone and done? Clean up?" Jess looked the newcomer up and down. Her hair was combed and it looked clean. She also had on clean clothes and they looked new.

The woman smiled. She took off her coat and wrapped it around Jess' shoulders. "I have been clean for a year now. I don't use and I don't need to use. I also accepted Jesus as my Lord and Savior. I get high on Him all the time. He's all I need."

"Aw, Kate. That's great." Jess' eyes wondered toward the man sitting on a nearby park bench. "I gotta go."

"Jess, come with me. Leave that stuff."

"I can't." Jess walked toward her next fix.

Jess was right. As long as she was living without Christ, she was a slave to the enemy. Satan had a hold on her that couldn't be stopped apart from God. Kate, however, was safe from Satan's clutches. She walked with the Lord, who protected her, as long as she walked close to Him.

Dear Lord, thank You for being my safe harbor in this world of sin and shame. Thank You for protecting me, for providing a safe place to go from the enemy. AMEN.

As a Child of God You are SIGNIFICANT

You are the salt of the earth. But if the salt loses its saltiness, how can it be made salty again? It is no longer good for anything except to be thrown out and trampled by men. You are the light of the world. A city on a hill cannot be hidden. Matt. 5:13-14

I Am Salt and Light of the Earth

Deborah took the turkey out of the fridge. She placed it in cold water in the sink to wait until she was ready for it. But first, she must make the dressing, her family's favorite treat for the Thanksgiving season.

"Sharon." She called her oldest daughter. "Bring me the salt, please."
"Salt. I hate salt." Her daughter, only ten years old, had a selective appetite and salt was not her favorite seasoning.
Deborah grinned. She knew her daughter would respond as she did but she was ready for her. "Do you know that we are salt and light in the world? The Bible says that believers are to be salt and light wherever they go."

"Yuck, I hate salt. I like the light though. Then I can read and see stuff." Sharon handed her

NOTES

mother the salt shaker. "Why does the Bible say we are salt and light?"

"Salt seasons, right? I mean, it adds flavor to food, even if you don't like it. Food would taste pretty bland if we didn't add some seasoning to it. God expects us to be that seasoning in our world, to remind people by our actions that He is alive and well. We are to affect those around us in a positive way just like the salt affects this dressing in a positive way. It adds to the flavor."

"But Mom...salt tastes funny and burns my lips."

"Yes it does when you eat it by itself. But if you add it to other food, it brings out the flavor." Deborah smiled. "God doesn't want us to blend in with the world around us but we should bring out the best flavor in people by living as He would have us live. Our actions tell louder than words what He wants others to know about Him."

Ok, I guess I understand that, I think but..." Sharon looked toward the ceiling fan where the light was coming from. "What about the light thing?"

"In Matthew 5:14, Jesus calls us

light of the world. He adds that a city on a hill cannot be hidden. Imagine this. Our city is on a huge hill. Do you think people can see it from a long way off?" Deborah loved these opportunities to teach her daughter God's truth.

"Sure, but..."

"If we don't speak about our faith, go along with the kids at school or pretend we aren't Christians, we're hiding our light. We are the light of God's truth to the people around us. We are to bring truth to people when the enemy would deceive them into believing a lie."

"Great mom, another Bible lesson and I fell right into it." Sharon hugged her mother. "I'll try to remember this one though. It sounds like we have been given a privilege and we'd better not mess it up."

"Sharon, let's always pray before you go out with your friends. That way we can keep each other on our toes."

Father, help me stay alert to the opportunities You present to be salt and light in my world. Help me speak words when I need to, be a good example, and share my faith diligently. AMEN.
"

NOTES

I am the true vine and my Father is the gardener. If a man remains in Me and I in him, he will bear much fruit; apart from Me you can do nothing. John 15:1,5b

I Am a Branch of the True Vine

Munn watched as her husband Drego planted another row of vines. They were vintners, makers of good wine or so they thought. Drego plopped another plant into the ground.

"Munn, come over here. I need you to hold this so I can add this graft." Drego selected another short branch from the supply near his elbow.

"What are you doing? Won't that hurt the vine to cut into it like that?" Munn held the vine tightly and watched as he made a tiny slit into the side of it.

Drego silently placed the cutting into the slit. "This graft will ensure that we have the best

wine for miles around next spring. As long as the graft is attached to the vine, it will produce great wine."

Drego and Munn didn't know it but they were demonstrating exactly what happens when we become children of God. We are grafted into the perfect vine, Jesus Christ, our Lord and Savior. As long as we allow God to teach us, to prune us, and extract impurities from us, we will flourish and draw others towards the light of God's truth. That's the fruit that God wants us to produce.

Have you ever watched a Christian man or woman who seems to attract people no matter where they go? People listen to them, follow their example, and want to be around them all the time. They are producing fruit, the kind of fruit that has eternal value; the kind of fruit that honors and glorifies God Almighty, and brings glory to the divine sacrifice that Jesus made when he died on the cross.

We are to be that kind of branch, grafted into the true vine, Jesus Christ, so that one day God will say, "Well done, good and faithful servant."

A friend of mine wrote a song depicting a man's entrance into the kingdom of heaven. The Lord meets him there and says,

> "Well done, good and faithful son, you have entered your rest. Well done, my devoted one. Your sacrifice has been

blessed"
One day, you will stand before the Lord in heaven. Will He say those words to you?

NOTES

Father, I am significant. I know that I can make a difference in the lives of those around me as long as I stay grafted in You. Please help me remember that I have a job to do, that I am to produce fruit. AMEN.

You did not choose Me but I chose you and appointed you to go and bear fruit – fruit that will last. Then the Father will give you whatever you ask in My name. John 15:16

I Am Chosen and Anointed to Bear Fruit

Danny walked into the gray-walled, sparsely furnished room and sat. His wait didn't last long. A door clanged. Keys rattled. In walked a tall man, gaunt in appearance, but full of pride. Two prison guards watched as his footsteps echoed across the bare room.

"Dad..." Danny moved to his father's side.

"Sh-h-h-h. Danny boy. Let's sit." The large man plunked his weight into the nearest metal chair. He wriggled uncomfortably as the cold metal bit through his thin clothing.

"But, dad," Danny whispered. "I can't let you do this. I can't." Danny's eyes welled with unshed tears.

"You can and you will boyo. I've chosen this. Now you accept it. And live the best life you can so I can be proud of you." Danny embraced the only man he'd ever loved. He looked deep into

NOTES

his father's eyes and knew there was no changing his mind once it was made up.

"Dad, I deserve to die, not you. That man, the one I shot..." His father placed a large hand over his son's mouth.

"You don't know if they're listening. Keep quiet. I love you son. I will do this one last thing for you. Now will you accept this and stay away from here. No more police. No more stealing. Promise me."

"I promise." Danny watched his father return the way he'd come. His tears streamed freely now, no shame for loving this man.

Jesus Christ made that choice for you. He chose to walk to His death, even though you were the one who deserved to die. Will you accept His gift? Will you live your life in payment by bearing fruit for Him, by bringing others into the kingdom, by living free from the bondage of sin?

Father God, thank You for giving me life through Your death. Help me bear fruit for Your kingdom and for Your glory. AMEN.

But you will receive power when the Holy Spirit comes on you and you will be My witnesses in Jerusalem, and in all of Judea and Samaria, and to the ends of the earth. Acts 1:8

I Am a Personal Witness of Christ

Jessy placed a frail hand on her granddaughter's arm. She squeezed as much as she could to let the young woman know she was awake and listening.

"Grandma, please, don't die." Deena's tears flowed freely. She had been sitting by her beloved grandmother's side for three days, watching the older woman grow weaker, sleep more, and breathe more laboriously.

"Deena, don't you know?" The frail voice was little more than a whisper. "Your memories will keep me with you for as long as you want. When you tell your children about me, my memory lives in them too." Jessy sighed, took one last shuddering breath, and then closed her eyes.

"Grandma, grandma." Deena shook her a little but knew that there was no use. Her grandmother had passed away. She laid her head on the bed beside the woman who had raised her, and wept uncontrollably for a

NOTES

few minutes but then remembered her grandmother's words. She would tell her children all the stories about growing up in this house, about the cooking lessons at her grandmother's side, and the games they'd played together. Her children would have a rich heritage because the grandmother had spent time with Deena and they would learn to appreciate that heritage.

Jesus has given us the significant task of telling others about Him, about His miracles, His lineage, His creation, everything so that they too will know that He loves them, died for them and wants to save them from the machinations of the enemy. Jesus is counting on us, to spread the Good News about His coming, His death and resurrection, and His eternal home beside the Father as our intercessor. Deena planned to tell her children about her grandmother and she was the only one who could since she'd lived those wonderful days with the elderly woman. Will you tell others about Jesus? Will you advance His Kingdom on earth?

Father God, I will faithfully keep you before anyone who comes across my path either by word or deeds, letting them know that you love them. Thank You for giving my life significance. AMEN.

Don't you know that you yourselves are God's temple and that God's Spirit lives in you?

1 Cor. 3:16

NOTES

I Am God's Temple

Duke walked across the parking lot, head bent, wondering what he'd find inside the clubhouse. The Bandeleros had been robbed, their stash of contraband cigarettes stolen, their trophies nowhere to be seen. He had a sneaking suspicion who the culprits were but he had no proof and without that...

"Hey Duke. You wanta ride, see if we can find 'em?" A large, rather hairy man stood just inside the door. Duke raised his hand in acknowledgment.

"Naw. They're long gone by now. Those trophies are irreplaceable. They probably smashed them or ditched them in some landfill. We worked hard to earn them but now they're gone for good." He rubbed his forehead, an achy feeling of depression filling the spaces in his brain.

Just as the Bandeleros were robbed in this story, so were the people of Jerusalem when Nebuchadnezzar, King of Babylon, ransacked their temple and kidnapped their youth. A young man named Daniel, was taken from his home along with all God's Holy vessels from the temple. The Babylonians treated Daniel fairly, for the most part, and they never touched the vessels, the temple trophies, until a king by the name of Belshazzar came to power. He took those goblets and used them during one of his drinking parties. God killed him that very night.

God considers you to be His temple, the Holy vessel containing His Holy Spirit. You are significant and He cares about you more than you even care about yourself. He loves you more than your parents ever did. You are irreplaceable to Him. Imagine!

He sent His Holy Spirit to live in you so that you would never have to face temptation alone again. The Holy Spirit seeks to sanctify you on a daily basis, to make you even more Holy.

Dear Lord, Thank You for considering me Your holy temple, Your holy vessel. Help me to see myself that way and to take care of myself in the future. AMEN.

NOTES

Therefore if anyone is in Christ, he is a new creation; the old has gone, the new has come. All this is from God who reconciled us to Himself through Christ and gave us the ministry of reconciliation that God was reconciling the world to Himself in Christ not counting men's sins against them. And He has committed to us the message of reconciliation. We are therefore Christ's ambassadors as though God were making His appeal through us. We implore you on Christ's behalf: be reconciled to God. God made Him who had no sin to be sin for us so that in Him we might become the righteousness of God. 2 Cor.5:17-21

I Am a Minister of Reconciliation for God

Trask entered the bar, searched the faces to see if he knew anyone and then proceeded to step up to the bar. “Give me a diet coke.” He placed a couple of dollar bills on the counter.

“Hey bud.” A large meaty hand grabbed his shoulder and Trask turned to face the man who’d stepped up beside him. “Gant, how’re you doin’?

“I’m ok. How ‘bout you?” Just as Trask was about to answer, the bartender plunked a can of coke down in front of him. He took a long thirsty swig and wiped the back of his hand across his mouth. “I’m better now,” he answered.

“What’s with the coke? Never seen you drink anything but beer.” Gant leaned his elbows on the scratched up surface and stared at their reflection in the mirror behind the liquor bottles. “You sick or something?”

“Naw. I’m finally clear of that stuff. I don’t even like the smell of it anymore. And I’ve never felt better.” Trask took another swig. He looked sideways, assessing his response in the face of his companion. Gant continued to stare straight ahead. “I found Jesus and I feel like a new man s’all.”

Gant turned his face toward Trask. The man didn’t appear to be as edgy anymore. But what about... “Hey you gone soft or something?” Gant ducked, waiting for the blow to come. No one called

NOTES

Trask soft.
"Naw, just changed." Trask smiled and turned to sit with his back leaning on the bar. If he'd been a girl, he'd giggle at the look on Gant's face.

People who have had a personal encounter with Jesus Christ are not just reformed, rehabilitated, or reeducated. They are re-created, new creatures, with all the old habits gone and new habits beginning to form. We become true individuals, with a new body, new perspectives, and new purpose.

Trask was the same on the outside, but inside, he felt better and treated his body better. And his mind was clear for the first time in a very long time. He no longer had angry outbursts. His friends would have to learn to respect the new man.

God creates within us a new perspective so we can walk with Him, talk to Him, and tap into His power to defend ourselves from the arrows of the enemy who seeks to kill and destroy us. He does this so others will be drawn to want what we have, the Lord Jesus Himself.

Father, thank you for renewing me on the inside and giving my life new purpose, for adding a skip to my step. Thank you for sending the SON to shine on my world. Help me be a worthy example of Your love to those around me. AMEN.

As God's fellow workers we urge you not to receive God's Grace in vain.

2 Cor. 6:1

NOTES

I Am God's Co-Worker

Gina worked her way through the smoke filled room toward the man who was bent over the pool table. Her hand carried a frosty glass of his favorite beer.

"Here, Jer, a cold one." She placed the glass on the wood edge surrounding the green felt. Jer scowled toward her as she moved to sit on the bench against the wall.

"Get this off here. How you think I can move with that there? Stupid...." He shouted the obscenity at her loud enough for everyone in the room to hear. Snickers could be heard from all corners as she timidly did his bidding.

Gina had been raised in a Christian home. She'd heard God's message of salvation many times and had even asked Jesus into her heart when she was a child. But her choices as an adult left many wondering if she'd ever truly made a commitment to Him at all.

She'd chosen to hang with a crowd of losers, boozers, and thieves who partied all the time, stealing to pay for their entertainment. She belonged to Jer, was his girlfriend, and so he passed her around sometimes and she let him. She didn't like it but that was life in this crowd. He only hit her anyway, if she refused to go along with it.

Gina ignored God's message as if the words had no power to change her life at all. The women and men in her social circle didn't know a thing about God and didn't want to. Gina was not an example any of them wanted to follow.

The Bible tells us not to receive God's Grace in vain. We are significant when we allow God to transform us, renewing our minds with His Word. Without it, we become chattel, the property of the enemy and all his followers. Seek to understand God's plans for you. Follow Him and the path of freedom will take you to high places, like heaven.

Lord, bless the words that you've spoken to my heart. Help them take root and change me. Help me not hear them in vain. AMEN.

And God raised us up with Christ and seated us with Him in the heavenly realms in Christ Jesus.
Eph. 2:6

NOTES

I Am Seated With Christ in Heaven

Ella scrubbed and scrubbed, her hands turning red with the effort. The floor gleamed, waxed to a high shine by the time she'd finished but her hands were cracked and bleeding. She quickly smoothed some antibiotic ointment on them and covered them with gloves but then continued toward the staircase to the bedrooms. It was almost 8 a.m. The family would soon be down for breakfast and she needed to tidy their rooms, make their beds and clean out their bathrooms before they finished.

Ella was a servant. Her masters treated her fairly but mostly, as if she didn't exist. They had friends, places to go, and things to do that were out of reach for Ella. She worked from sunup to sundown, every day, hoping that one day her life would change.

One morning, a messenger came by. He extended the King's invitation to a party to celebrate his son's birthday. Have you figured out the story? Cinderella, of course. She ended up married to the prince and living happily ever after.

God has placed us next to His Son in the heavenly realms. We join Christ in God's Kingdom when we ask Jesus to be the center of our life. We are elevated by the King of Kings and Lord of Lords and given a place of prominence just like Cinderella. Only this is not a fairy tale, a piece of fiction written about by mortal men or women. This is God's truth and it's available to all of us, not just one lonely young girl.

Father, thank you for seating me with Christ in Your Heavenly Kingdom. Thank You for thinking me significant enough to belong in Your house and by Your side. AMEN.

For we are God's workman-ship, created in Christ Jesus to do good works, which God prepared in advance for us to do. Eph. 2:10

NOTES

I Am God's Workmanship

Elma dipped her brush into the perfect color of paint for the blue hues she wanted to create on the canvas. She'd been working all morning to adapt a photo she'd taken last week to a masterpiece, a work of art that her client had asked for. Elma sighed. This was going to take a long time but then, the money was worth it. Her paintings were sold for a great deal of money these days, considered collector's items.

Elma, an artist using the oil medium, had earned the right to be considered one the best artists in her city, or even in her country. People from all over the world commissioned work from her and were willing to pay exorbitant fees and wait inordinate amounts of time. This current pro-

ject would be considered her finest workmanship.

God is our creator. We are His workmanship, created in Christ to do good works, a work He prepared ahead of time for us to do. We don't just hang on God's walls for other people or angels to look at. We have a job to do, a job that gives our life meaning and purpose.

Do you consider the work God has for you to do each day? How do you accomplish what He has set for you to do? Do you just go about your business ignoring what God's plans are for you? Maybe today, you might want to ask God what He wants and then do it.

Father, you created me for a purpose, gave me significance in that task. Thank You. Help me do it to the best of Your ability for without You Lord, I am hopeless to the cause. AMEN.

In Him and through faith in Him we may approach God with freedom and confidence.

Eph. 3:12

NOTES

I Am free to Approach God with Confidence

"Hey, Red, wanna come with me to the Blaine residence? They got a party goin' on." TJ looked expectantly toward his current girlfriend.

Sherie continued to look out the window. Her red hair sparkled in the sun's reflection through the panes of glass. "I don't know those people. That big house scares me. What if I touch something and it breaks. Everything in there must cost a fortune." Sherie turned towards her boyfriend. "We don't fit with those people."

TJ grinned. "I got a personal invitation from the man himself. He likes me. We get along."

Sherie shrugged her thin shoulders. Her t-shirt, beads attached to the frayed hem, made a clicking sound as she moved. "Are you sure he meant for us to come when all his friends were there?"

"Sure, come on. You'll have fun."

TJ was Sherie's ticket into a home that she'd dreamed about for a long time. When she was a child, she'd pass the house and wonder about the people who lived inside. She pretended that one day she'd have a home just like that and children whom she'd love unconditionally.

Jesus is our ticket to the father's side. Because of His death on the cross, His payment for the sin debt we owed, we have the freedom to approach God with confidence. God sees us as significant because of the price Christ paid on the cross. All we have to do is believe.

We don't even have to get in our car and drive over there as Sherie and TJ had to do. We can sit in our own homes and reach out to our Creator, our Father in heaven.

Lord, Thank you for making me significant in the Father's eyes. Thank You for interceding on my behalf and allowing God to see me as white as snow. AMEN.

I can do everything through Him who gives me strength.
Phil. 4:13

NOTES

I Can do Anything with Christ

Janet trembled. Going to this particular rally frightened her to death. What if...but then she'd already dealt with the what if's. She turned them over to God, hadn't she? This was still way out of her comfort zone. Maybe...

Just then, Jason, her husband, roared up to the front door on his shiny black and chrome Harley. He was raring to go, excited to show his new bike to the other members of the group they'd be camping with. Sometimes, Janet thought he loved that bike more than her...but only sometimes.

Jason grinned toward her, a silly smirk, excitement shiny from every pore of his skin. He began loading their gear into the saddle bags, the trunk and on the top of the trunk. Janet watched as he secured everything with bungees as she reluctantly strapped her helmet in place. Jason would never understand if she said she didn't want to go again.

"Come on hon. Let's boogie." Jason waited patiently for Janet to straddle the bike and sit in the passenger seat. He got on and then they connected their headphones so they could talk to each other while they rode. "Let's pray, Janet, before we head out."

Jason bowed his head and Janet followed his example. She listened as he began to talk to His Lord. "Father, this ministry is your idea and you have called us to participate in it with you. Please protect us as we drive, and protect us at the rally. Keep us sensitive to those You bring into our path so we can minister with Your love to them all. Also Father, calm Janet. Help her see that with You we can do all things for it's Your strength we are tapped into. AMEN."

Janet understood, but had yet to experience, the peace that passes understanding when we walk where God wants us to walk. It is through Him and with Him that we can do whatever He asks us to do as He takes us out of our comfort zones. We are significant to His plan for the people on this earth and all we have to do is walk in His footsteps.

Father, take me out of my comfort zone so I can experience Your peace in all circumstances. Help me be aware of where You want me to go and then help me be obedient to follow. AMEN.

NOTES

Is any one of you in trouble? He should pray. Is anyone happy? Let him sing songs of praise. Is anyone of you sick? He should call the elders of the church to pray over him and anoint him with oil in the name of the Lord. And the prayer offered in faith will make the sick person well; the Lord will raise him up. If he has sinned he will be forgiven. Therefore confess your sins to each other and pray for each other so that you may be healed. The prayer of a righteous man is powerful and effective. James 5:13-16

I am a Prayer Warrior for my Friends

Dell walked toward the stone structure he'd come to call his home church. He reflected on the way his life had changed since he'd become a believer. It wasn't that long ago that he had few friends and the ones he considered friends were only his friend as long as he had booze or dope to feed them.

He'd lived in a biker gang, partying all the time at their meeting place, a local bar that was still there but of no interest to him now. In fact, one of the guys had called him yesterday.

“Hey, Dell, where you been buddy. We missed ya.” The voice had sounded raspy to Dell’s ear, the dry sound of a smoker who’d coughed up a storm recently.

Dell smiled into the receiver. “I been around. How’re you doin’? Still smokin’ I see. Those things’ll kill you one of these days.”

The caller suppressed another cough. “Still preachin’ I see. That’ll get you dead one of these days.” The threat was evident in the menacing sound that reached Dell’s ears. He’d crossed the line.

“Hey Dell.” The caller continued as if he’d never spoken harshly. “Wanna come to the ‘Spokes’? We could have a few laughs just like the old days.” He cleared his throat a few times and then laughed in a forced manner.

“Naw. I quit that place. You know that. But the place where I go now is a friendly place and you’d be welcome.” Dell stopped breathing waiting for an answer.

A loud incredulous laugh rang through the phone waves. “Me? Go to church? It is church you’re talking about, ain't it? I heard you got religion. Leave me outta that, man. I don't need none of that." The phone went dead. It was as if the caller raced to get away from something that was chasing him.

Dell walked on. He recalled the feeling of hopelessness that he'd felt then but also the knowledge that God could change that man as he'd changed him. Dell also remembered how the pastor urged his congregation to not take rejection personally but to continue to pray for the people God placed on their heart. Dell also added his friend to the prayer chain. He had many others praying for his friend now.

Dell was not alone. His church family celebrated life with him, prayed with him, and invited him to many fun get-togethers. Dell had even met a wonderful woman who didn't care what he'd done a couple of years ago. She loved the man he was now.

Being part of the family of God gives us a whole new group of friends who really do care about us both physically and spiritually. Are you part of a believing congregation? Do you pray for them and do you ask them to pray for you? Do they keep you accountable? We are all significant to the people we attend church with as we pray, fellowship, and keep each other on the narrow path toward heaven.

Father, thank You for my friends. Thank you for bringing me to this fellowship of believers and for the freedom we have to meet together and praise you together every week. AMEN.

NOTES

As a child of the Father in heaven, our Creator, You are FREE

He stilled the storm to a whisper; the waves of the sea were hushed.
Psalm 107:29

Freedom From Fear

Fear, that indelible stain on life that paralyzes, was not a word that Paul ever used out loud but one that caused his stomach to churn and his breathing to labor at the worse times. His cellmate however slept like a baby.

"Hey, man. You hear that?" Paul shook him.

Jeff opened his eyes and glanced around. "What's happening?" He rubbed sleep from the corners of his mouth and sat on the edge of his bunk. "You stoned or somethin'?"

"Yeah, right. I'm just sittin' here listenin' to all that ruckus and smokin up a storm. You hear that? Those cons could decide they want us wit them and then what. We get busted right along wit them." Paul moved as far away from the bars as he could, trying hard to become invisible.

Jeff just lay back down. "The Lord is on my side so who can be against me? That's what I learned yesterday when that biker guy came for Bible study. I never thought I'd join a group like that but He knew what he was talkin' about. I got Jesus now so I don't need to worry about nothin'."

NOTES

"Jesus, how's that dude make a difference when He's dead. He couldn't save himself from those Roman guys nailing Him to a cross. How's He supposed to save us? Huh? Tell me that? We got no one but ourselves."

Jeff had learned that with Christ we can be free from fear and worry. Imagine sleeping through a prison riot! What's keeping you awake at night? What steals your joy and keeps you bound by fear? Fear is like chains, binding, making it impossible for you to walk where God wants you to walk. Whether fear of criminals, finances, animals, illness, whatever clogs your pores so that sleep eludes you, give it to Jesus, the one who calms the storms in life.

Father, calm my storm. Take away my fear and give me freedom to enjoy life and my walk with You. AMEN.

Therefore I tell you do not worry about your life, what you will eat or drink; or about your body, what you will wear. Is not life more important than food and the body more important than clothes? Matthew 6:25

Freedom From Worry

Jennifer walked towards her mother, the latter displaying an anxious expression of worry. "Mom, what's wrong?"

"I can't seem to stop worrying about how to pay those bills your father left when he died. How in the world am I going to get that much money?" Mary sat down heavily on the sofa, waiting for her daughter to join her.

"Mother, I told you it would work out. I know you're used to having all these things done for you but I will teach you how to budget...and besides, has worrying helped with the problem?"

"No, but..." Mary fidgeted.

Jennifer sighed. Her mother was a worrywart. She had driven her father nuts

NOTES

sometimes even though he was supposed to be looking after the finances and such. Of course, she reflected, maybe mother should have gotten involved so she'd know how bad things had gotten.

"Mom, concern spurs us to action but worry can damage your health, disrupt your productivity, affect the way you treat others in a negative way, and reduce your ability to trust in God. Can we agree that worry is not the way to go? Let's use our concern to formulate a plan of action. Ok?" Jennifer took out a scratch pad and together they began to plan.

As Christians we are told not to worry. In fact, we have the freedom to leave things in God's hands. allow Him to stimulate our thought processes and form a plan of action when situations require it. Mary found she could not concentrate, think productively, or move beyond her worry. Worry debilitated her.

Freedom from worry allows us to have a good night's sleep so our rested body can function the next day and our thinking is clear. Freedom from worry means we place our trust in God, depend on Him for answers and seek His good for our life in every situation. Freedom from worry about what others think, allows us to be the person God created us to be.

Father, thank You that I can be the person you created me to be. Thank You for the freedom from worry and for taking care of my needs, whether through a plan of action I've devised with Your help or through someone else. AMEN.

NOTES

And so we know and rely on the love God has for us. God is love. Whoever lives in love lives in God and God in him. There is not fear in love. But perfect love drives out fear because fear has to do with punishment. The one who fears is not made perfect in love. 1 John 4: 16, 18

Freedom From Wrong Thinking

Donna carefully lifted the old woman from her chair to her bed. "Volunteering for this job could end up giving me back problems for the rest of my life," she thought not for the first time. "Earning brownie points, just earning brownie points."

Donna finished her job that day, let in the volunteer that worked the night shift and got into her car to head home. She'd just have time to get to the supermarket before she'd have to start dinner. As she parked the car in the lot near her favorite store, she noticed a long time friend exiting her car. "Jess, how are you?" she hollered across the asphalt.

"Donna, Hi. It's so good to see you. How's it going?" Jessica walked over towards her friend and hugged her. They walked toward the store together. "What are you doing these days?"

"I'm volunteering for an old lady who's recovering from surgery. I hope the Lord appreciates what I do for Him. I hope it's enough." Donna straightened her back to accent the tiredness she felt.

"What do you mean?" Jess stopped walking and looked at her friend.

"Well, we know that if we don't serve others, God will get mad at us and punish us when we die...judgments remember?"

"So, let me get this straight. You're helping out this old woman because you fear that if you don't, God will punish you on judgment day?"

"Yeah, well, the Bible says we have to do good works, doesn't it?" Donna began to get huffy. She was tired and didn't need to justify why she did things.

"But Donna, God wants us to do good things because He did a good thing for us...when He died on the cross. Our good deeds should reflect our gratitude. We do them not because we have to but because we want to. Your fear of God's punishment is coloring the way you treat people, isn't it? I'll bet you resent this woman."

NOTES

"Yeah well...I've read about God's judgment. It's..."

"Not for us. As Christians, we do not have to face God's White Throne judgment since our name is in the Lamb's Book of Life. We are free from His judgment. You accepted Christ into your heart the same time I did. I know you're a Christian. Now live like it." She hooked her arms through Donnas and together they walked into the grocery store.

"It's good to talk with you again. We need to do this more often." Donna chuckled. "You always did keep me on the straight and narrow."

Donna was living under fear that God would punish her if she did not do good deeds. How much would be enough to satisfy God anyway? Jesus satisfied God when He died for our sins on the cross. We don't need to earn heaven. All we need is to believe and then live a life of gratitude for what He did for us.

Father, thank you for satisfying my debt, for dying for my sin. I am grateful. Help me live like it and leave fear exactly where it belongs, at Satan's feet. AMEN.

NOTES

Be self controlled and alert. Your enemy the devil prowls around like a roaring lion looking for someone to devour. Resist him, standing firm in the faith, because you know that your brothers throughout the world are undergoing the same kind of sufferings. 1 Peter 5:8-9

Freedom From Satan's Deception

Gloria leaned against the doorframe to the living room. "There he sits," she mused to herself, "gut hanging out of his pants, snoring so loudly that you'd have to turn up the television if you wanted to hear anything, and he hasn't trimmed his beard in a week. Barry comes home from work and just sits there. Great husband he is."

Gloria spent her afternoon watching soap operas. The men were clean cut, handsome, some were scoundrels but most were romantic and fine. In comparison, her husband didn't stand a chance. Barry had never hit her in their 25 years of marriage. He worked hard to provide a nice house with enough food for the family to eat and clothes for them to wear. He always remembered her birthday and he never treated her with anything other than respect but Gloria was dissatisfied.

The enemy is prowling as 1 Peter 5:8 says, to seek, kill, and destroy. Instead of concentrating on her husband's good points, Gloria was thinking only about the things Barry didn't do or the way he looked after a hard day working construction.

There are some good reasons for women to leave their husbands. These are not some of them. Dissatisfaction is like a cancer. Speak it out loud to a few friends, who also share their frustrations and before you know it, you've given yourself permission to get a divorce.

Women are legendary for sniping about their husbands to other women. We need to build our husbands up, not tear them down in front of other people. If you catch yourself doing it, stop. Remember He was your choice to marry making Him God's choice for you. Choose instead to have a happy marriage. Overlooking the small things he doesn't do and concentrate on the big sacrifices he makes to support you.

Father, my husband is your choice for me. Help me respect him in the manner you want me to because I love you, not because he deserves it. AMEN.

NOTES

You will keep in perfect peace him whose mind is steadfast because he trusts in you.
Isaiah 26:3

Freedom From Worry

Sam listened but had a hard time believing that his reprieve was over. Seven years earlier, he'd been diagnosed with an aggressive type of cancer with a 1% survival rate. He'd battled and won and now seven years later it was back. How was he going to tell Diane?

He walked out of the doctor's office, moved toward his SUV and sat down on the driver's seat hard. Would he make it this time? Is this the end for him?

Plugging his key into the ignition, he turned the vehicle on and shifted into drive mechanically, his mind elsewhere. The scenario of a conversation with Diane just two weeks ago began to play in his head. They'd been thanking God for the years he'd been given and now...

Sam drove towards his office building. It was still the middle of the day, too early to head home. He wanted to talk to Diane so badly. She knew he'd had this other appointment

NOTES

and that the doctor was worried after his last check-up. He didn't want to tell her over the phone.

Sam turned down a side street. He picked up his cell phone. "Dan." He spoke when his boss answered. "I need to go home. I need to discuss the findings from the doctor with Diane and I can't do it over the phone." Sam turned the vehicle toward home.

"That bad huh? I'll see you tomorrow then. We'll be praying for you Sam." He hung up and Sam reflected on God's gift to him of a Christian boss. All the way home, he saw how God had gifted him with many blessings over the last seven years. He'd even been able to see his first grandson.

When he pulled into the driveway, Diane opened the front door, concern written all over her face. She knew without Sam telling her that the news was not good. Tears welled in her eyes but she swiped them away quickly before Sam saw them. He hated to see her cry over him.

They hugged for a long time when Sam entered their home. Then Diane made a pot of tea and the conversation began. "God has looked after me so far and given me seven wonderful years. He will see us through this too." Sam looked hopefully toward Diane, trying to infuse his optimism into her psyche.

"Our ladies Bible study is in the book of Daniel. We're learning that God saves us from the fire, saves us through the fire and saves us by the fire. No matter the outcome, God will save you." Tears flowed freely now at the thought of God taking her husband but Diane loved the Lord and knew He loved her unconditionally. God also loved Sam.

"Trusting in God means that whatever the outcome, we will keep our eyes on Him, right? That's how we'll handle this new situation." Sam reminded Diane of God's blessings and together, they began to plan for a fight, to do battle with cancer once again, with God's help.

Father, help me keep my eyes on You no matter what the circumstances are in my life. Build my trust today Lord, so that when I need it, it will be strong. AMEN.

NOTES

The Lord will guide you always; He will satisfy your needs in a sun-scorched land and will strengthen your frame. Isaiah 58:11a

Freedom From Wrong Choices

Trudy walked slowly toward the rally entrance, her car locked in the designated parking lot. Her campsite had been set up the night before so today she could concentrate on walking where the Lord guided her. Today, she was tuned into the people around her.

One young lady arrived at the entrance, seated on the tiny back seat of a motorcycle driven by a large, definitely older man. She hopped off as soon as the bike stopped and rubbed her sore backside. Her face was sun scorched and her hair, tied into a braid, was wind whipped, in need of a comb.

Trudy was close enough to hear their verbal exchanges. "Get me a cold drink of water, will ya?" The man sat with one leg crossed over the gas tank of his bike. His long beard look tattered and when he removed his head rag, the line between sunburn and bare scalp was clearly visible giving him the appearance of a skin colored cap. The woman moved quickly to comply.

Trudy lowered her head and watched. When the woman returned, the man took one sip and then threw the bottle at her. "That's not cold, b----. Get me a cold one." Trudy cringed as the woman retraced her steps to retrieve another bottle of water. Why do women put up with this kind of treatment, she asked herself and then continued on her way toward her campsite, a distance down the road.

During the course of the weekend, there were several times when Trudy saw the same woman. Her young, very pretty countenance was always sober looking. No sign of a smile was ever witnessed by anyone in the Christian group Trudy worked with. She'd asked them all to pray for this woman as soon as she'd entered camp. Everyone made a point to smile toward the woman whenever they could.

Late Saturday night, just before group members went toward their separate tents to attempt some sleep in that raucous atmosphere, the young woman

NOTES

stumbled toward them. She had several bruises on her face and arms and tears slid uncontrollably down her cheeks. “Manny’s looking for me and I can’t let him find me. Can I sleep here tonight?”

Trudy straightened from the opening to her tent. “Lord, please let me share your love with this woman tonight,” she whispered as she turned toward the woman. “You can share my tent.”

“Oh, I don’t need to sleep in your tent. Just let me sleep on the ground somewhere. Anywhere, as long as Manny can’t find me.” Her lips trembled and she rubbed the bruises on her right arm tenderly.

“No way.” Trudy went over and hugged her. “I have a large mattress, a queen size actually. I also have some clean sweats and I think we’re about the same size. Come on, let’s get some sleep.” She hooked her arm around the shoulders of this young person in a comforting manner.

That night Trudy was able to lead Tracey into the Kingdom as she explained how Jesus had died for her sins. The Lord strengthened

Tracey that night, satisfied her need for protection. The next day she went home alone. She resolved to find a Bible believing church with the help of members from a Christian motorcycle group who happened to live near her. Tracey clung to God's promises from a small pamphlet that Trudy gave her.

Are you being sensitive, like Trudy, for opportunities to share Christ's love and God's promises with someone today? Furthermore, are you relying on God to strengthen you and to guide you when you leave home or through trials and situations? God wants to free you with His love as you follow where He leads.

Father God, thank You for loving me and for loving all those whom You will send my way today. Help me keep my eyes focused on You and Help me shine with Your love as I greet and meet others. AMEN.

Consider how the lilies grow. They do not labor or spin. Yet I tell you, not even Solomon in all his splendor was dressed like one of these. Luke 12:27

NOTES

Freedom From Discontent

Diane looked at yet another catalogue. They kept coming in the mail, even from places she'd never heard of. This one wanted to sell her some new leather chaps and vest. The one yesterday wanted her to redecorate, or at least, add to her furnishings. The temptation to buy more was incredible.

She looked around her modest home toward the lumpy looking mass of fur lying on the rug by her back door. "Boomer, we need anything?" She always talked to her favorite pet during the day when there was no one else to bounce ideas off. The dog's ears perked up for a second but then relaxed in sleep once more. "You're no help."

Diane continued to

look around. She really did have everything she needed. Sometimes she'd like a newer dish-washer or a stove with all four burners working but she only ever used the front two anyway. Contentment was a word that her pastor had preached on last Sunday.

He'd used Luke 12:27 to highlight his point. "Why should we keep striving for more and more when God supplies our needs," he'd said. "The world around us has become so materialistic. Nothing satisfies us anymore. Contentment is a lost art. If our needs are met by the Lord Himself, as this verse says, then what more could we really want?"

Diane put the catalogue down. There was nothing she needed. Her chaps and vest were still in good shape and besides she was dieting. Soon she'd be looking for a smaller size anyway. And as far as her house was concerned, she had a comfortable place, plenty of food to eat, and her constant companion, Boomer. She looked toward him again. "You sure know how to exude contentment, don't you Boomer? As long as you're fed and come for walks with me, you're happy. Me too," she said. "Me too."

Do you get caught up in the materialism of today's modern Babylon? The excessive spending, excessive debt, and excessive lifestyles of Babylon in the days of Daniel are evident in our western culture today. Learn to be content with what God has given you. Stick those catalogues in the garbage before they tempt you further to add to your debt load.

NOTES

Father help me with Your strength in the face of today's temptations. Keep the enemy, who wants to destroy me, at bay, bound and ineffective. Help me gird myself with Your sword, the Word of Your truth. AMEN.

But the angel said to them, "Do not be afraid. I bring you good news of great joy that will be for all people.
Luke 2:10

Freedom From Fear

"Ken, have you checked the doors? Make sure they're locked and turn the alarm on before you come to bed, ok?" Ginni lay under the covers, pulled them all the way up toward her chin, and listened. She could hear the long drawn out sigh of frustration coming from down the hall as her husband retraced his steps to do as she wanted again tonight.

Three weeks ago their house had been broken into when they'd been visiting their daughter. Now Ginni was afraid all the time. She thought she heard a noise just outside their bedroom window. "Ken, someone's outside!"

Fear can paralyze us, make us ineffective for our family and for the Lord. It can cause some people to barricade themselves inside their homes. They never venture out to meet people, to serve others, or even attend church. Fear can cause some to overlook the perfect job because it may involve flying around the country and they fear flying. It can cause a wife to re-

main behind when her husband wants to ride his motorcycle for fear of being in an accident.

NOTES

The Bible tells us that fear is not from God. Satan uses it to keep us from becoming the person God intends for us to be. He wins when we give in to those niggling tremors that disappear if only we'd trust God and take that first step out of our comfort zone.

In Luke, an angel appeared to shepherds watching their flocks of sheep on a hillside outside Bethlehem. If they had not listened to the angel, look what they would have missed. Joseph was also told not to fear when he was to take Mary as his wife even though she was pregnant. Look what he would have missed if he had not listened. Mary, too, was told not to fear, and God allowed her to be the mother of His Son.

What great opportunities are you missing just because you fear doing something that you've never done before or because you fear stepping into that environment? Focus your attention on the Lord Himself.

Step out of your comfort zone and watch what He does through you.

Lord, I do fear sometimes. Help me trust that You know what is best and will protect me if I walk where You want me to walk. Help me be the person You want me to be and the vessel that You can use for Your glory. AMEN.

NOTES

Come to Me, all you who are weary and burdened, and I will give you rest.

Matthew 11:28

Freedom From Over commitment

Janet buckled the baby into his car seat, slammed the door of the small SUV her husband just bought her, and sat in the driver's seat. For the next three hours, she was the family taxi driver. She sighed, tired already.

Jeremy had soccer practice, Louise had dance team practice, and Joan had swim lessons. Those she'd stay for since they were over first and then she'd retrace her route to pick everyone up. Supper was in the crockpot so they'd be able to quickly eat before driving over to watch Jeremy's baseball game.

After she got home tonight, she still had to get ready for her luncheon tomorrow (she was the speaker), and then the BPW meeting tomorrow night. "Yikes, I'd better think of someone to pick up the kids. I'll need to prepare another slow cooked meal. God bless the invention of the crockpot." Her mind whirled with activity as she drove toward the kid's school.

Busy-ness is one of Satan's tools to seek, devour, and destroy God's people. Parents, and grandparents as well, are so busy today that they have no time for family, little time for the Lord who seems to get their leftovers most of the time, and little time for their marriages.

Women and men too, want it all. We want all the material possessions that the world says we need, social standing in the community, and kids who excel at everything. Grandparents continue to seek new adventures, volunteer for one more community project, and race from one coffee get-together to another forgetting that the Lord sits quietly in their living room waiting to visit with them.

God's word cautions us against too many busy projects in our life. Even though sports activities are good for the kids, too many can cause them to get their priorities out of whack just like their parents, who rush here and rush there continually. We stick God on the back burner, fitting Him in here and there, if we have time. Most days we forget about Him altogether.

Do you think Satan enjoys your

NOTES

busy-ness? You can bet your boots he does and he'll continue to salve your conscience with how important this is and how important that is until God is a distant memory. What activities could you retire from your agenda so you can add quality time with God to the plan for your life?

Lord, I have been busy. Help me free my schedule so I can work where You want me to work and when You want me to sit quietly, help me make that a priority. I love You Lord, and want to be with You. Help me start my day, resting in Your Word and in conversation with You. AMEN.

But the fruit of the Spirit is love, joy, peace, patience, kindness, goodness, faithfulness, gentleness, and self-control. Against such things there is not law. Those who belong to Christ Jesus have crucified the sinful nature with its passions and desires.

Gal. 5:22-24

Freedom From Anger

Sherie's face was fused with the red hue of anger, loud obnoxious, out of control anger. Saliva leaked from the corners of her mouth as she spit hateful words towards her son. His body crumpled, shoulders sagged, and his eye-sight flew in all directions looking for a place of reprieve.

"But mom..."

"Forget it. I don't know how I could have given birth to such an ignorant boy." Sherie spat the words and stomped off to her bedroom sure that if she stayed in that room one more minute, she'd strike. She would not abuse her child as she'd been abused.

Sherie didn't realize it, or maybe she did but was not about to admit. She did abuse her son verbally, every time she treated him

NOTES

in this manner. She also believed that her Irish heritage was responsible for her angry outbursts and there was nothing she could do about it.

Sherie had a host of excuses after each incident. She was a Christian and knew that God wanted her to stop yelling and parent in a calm manner but, "This is just how I am," she'd say.

One day, a friend was visiting. Her son walked into the house she'd just cleaned with muddy boots. Sherie was livid. This time she didn't hide her anger. She just let it fly. Her friend was astounded.

"Sherie, stop. Do you know what you just said to Justin? How can you treat him that way?"

"What? Did you see what he did? I can't let him get away with that. What kind of parent would I be?" Sherie huffed, crossed her arms over her chest and stood as if waiting for her friend to apologize.

"Aren't you a Christian?"

"You know I am. The Bible

says…"

"Yes, the Bible says we are the branches tied into the vine of Holy God Almighty. We are to produce the fruit of…"

"Yeah, yeah. Patience, kindness, goodness, gentleness, etcetera, etcetera, etcetera. But I get so angry. It's that Irish blood, you know. We're hot heads."

"You can stop. What do you think happens to the Holy Spirit, residing in you, when you spout off like that? What do you suppose is His purpose in your life anyway?"

Sherie sat down hard. "I know that I grieve the Holy Spirit when I get angry. I want to be a Godly woman but every time Jason does one of his stupid stunts, I see red." Tears began to filter through her long eyelashes. "I hate the look on Jason's face when I lose control."

"Then when you feel yourself getting angry, stop. Get down on your knees and throw yourself at the foot of the throne of Grace. You are grafted into the power of God through the Holy Spirit so you can do anything He sets your heart to do with His help."

Sherie listened to her friend that day. Slowly over the next year, she practiced praying instead of blowing off steam. She became a calmer woman and Jason began to hug her once in a while as he'd done when he was little. Their home became more peaceful.

NOTES

Have you excused poor behavior as part of your heritage, or because it's expected of you? How often do you abuse the very ones you love the most by shouting obscenities or hateful words expecting it to bounce off them as soon as you've calmed down. It doesn't bounce off. In fact the Bible talks a lot about the damage our tongue can do. Let the Holy Spirit produce His fruit in your life. It's your choice.

Father, I am so sorry for grieving the Spirit with my anger. Please forgive my bad behavior. Holy Spirit remind me, every time I feel anger rise, to stop and seek Your help. AMEN.

If you then, though you are evil, know how to give good gifts to your children, how much more will your father in heaven give good gifts to those who ask Him. Matt. 7:11

Freedom From Worry

Josh was in trouble. He'd tried to stop his wife from leaving, grabbed her arm, and now he was sitting in jail, charged with spousal abuse. He had one phone call.

"Dad, I'm in jail. Melly filed a charge against me for abuse. She left me and took the kids. I tried to stop her and..." His voice shook. His fear was a tangible force that covered the distance between the jail and his parent's home.

His dad spoke slowly; making sure his words of comfort could be heard. "It's okay son. We'll be there as soon as we can."

Josh sighed in relief. His parents would know what to do. His wife had taken all the money in their bank account so he didn't even have any to post bail. A tear slid down his cheek, one that he quickly wiped away in case someone saw him crying like a baby. It would take a few hours but his parents were coming.

NOTES

Josh's dad dropped whatever he was doing, loaded the car, and drove hundreds of miles to support his son. Josh knew that whatever he asked them to do, his parents would do to the best of their ability. He felt secure in that knowledge. However, Josh's dad had limits. He was human and basically a sinner, just like Josh.

God is our heavenly Father more capable than any human father. He gives to His children all that He has so they can succeed in carrying out the work of spreading the gospel, whatever form that takes. When we accept Christ's gift of eternal life, walk where God wants us, He will provide the resources and the physical strength to carry our His wishes. We don't have to wonder if whatever comes into our life will destroy us. God loves us so much; He knows about our needs before we need them. His resources are limitless.

Do you wonder where your next meal will come from or where you're going to find the money to pay the debts you carry? What about an illness? Does the worry about it keep you from finding any joy in your life today? God loves you more than is possible for human parents or friends. Walk secure in that knowledge. Keep your eyes on heaven and walk where God places you, in confidence.

Father, thank You for giving me access to Your resources, for loving me so much that I can depend on You to provide for my needs. Help me keep my eyes focused on You today. Help me trust in Your love, Lord. AMEN.

NOTES

Therefore do not lose heart. Though outwardly we are wasting away, yet inwardly we are being renewed day by day. For our light and momentary troubles are achieving for us an eternal glory that far outweighs them all.
2 Cor. 4: 16-17

Freedom From the Past

Rachel grasped the piano leg, waiting for the next blow. Her father's leather belt had a large shiny buckle that bit into her skin every time it made contact with her bare legs. Rachel tried not to care, tried not to feel, and tried not to cry. Crying usually made the beatings worse.

Thus was the childhood of Jeremy's mother. But he never knew that about her. His mom was the kindest, most gentle woman he knew. He knew a few women from school who were not so kind. His mom tugged at his hat, making sure his ears were covered before he went outside. He blushed, sometimes wishing she'd not fuss so much, but then he'd hear about some of the moms his friends had and was thankful all over again for her fussing.

""I love you Jeremy." Jeremy peeked through his half closed eyes to watch as his mom waved toward him. He tried to appear not to notice but smiled all the same, feeling the warmth of her love course through his body. He skipped down the sidewalk.

Rachel had been abused from the time she was three months old. How she survived is anyone's guess but survive she did. Some days, she'd ask God to take her to heaven, to rescue her from a house where drugs and alcohol, parties and orgies were the norm. But God never did or so she thought way back then.

Now, she knew better. God had rescued her. He'd rescued her mind, body and soul for His purposes, renewing her into the person He wanted her to be. Today she was a mom and a great wife. At least that's what her husband told her once in a while, teasing that he didn't want her to get a swelled head. She loved being a mom, cherished the memories that her little family were making each day and supported her husband in the dreams he had for his life.

Do you harbor memories from a less than perfect childhood? Did your home depict the seedier side of life? God can take what you see as something that will destroy you and turn it into something that transforms you into the child He wants you to be, if you'll let Him.

NOTES

Father, thank you for rescuing me from my past. Thank You for changing me through my circumstances and drawing me into the comfort of Your Grace and Love. AMEN.

If you hold to My teaching, you are really My disciples. Then you will know the truth and the truth will set you free. John 8:31b-32

Freedom To Know Truth

Fay was a trusting person, or at least, that's the excuse she gave when Tyke left her in the middle of the night a week ago. He'd told her he loved her and wanted to marry her as soon as they could so she moved in with him. Now he was gone and he hadn't even said good-bye.

"Joan, I don't know why I let myself get into these situations?" Fay dropped her head into her arms that lay crossed on the kitchen table. "I trusted him. I loved him, I think, but I never thought he'd leave." Swollen eyes looked beseechingly toward Joan, a friend who'd recently come to know and love Jesus.

Joan cleared her throat. Would Fay listen this time? "Fay, I don't know too many people I'd trust the way I trust my Lord."

"What do you mean? You can't even see Him. How can you trust someone you can't see?" Fay hiccupped and then blew her nose.

Joan settled back into her chair. This could take awhile, she thought. "Jesus is alive and I have faith that He loves me and died for my sins on the cross. I know he's real because I'm not the same person I used to be. Remember how I used to smoke, drink, chase the guys?"

"You mean like I do?" Fay sniffled.

Joan grinned. "Yeah, like you do. Anyhow, I hate the smell of smoke, I don't need no booze any more, and I look at the guys we hang with through the eyes of Jesus. They aren't all that good for us. Most of them don't even have a full time job. All they do with any paycheck is blow it on booze and drugs. Like Tyke did."

Fay sat back in her chair and eyed her friend. She knew Joan was telling her the truth. Why couldn't she have known that Tyke wasn't trustworthy? "Does this God of yours give you smarts so you know who to trust and who not to?"

Joan's eyes widened. Finally. "Fay, God has provided us with a large book called the Bible. In it is all the truth we'll ever need. Do you want to ask Jesus to come into your heart and change you into the person He wants you to be?"

Fay nodded. "Will he help me get a new boyfriend?" She chuckled. She knew she wasn't ready for another relationship and from now on, she'd consult God's truth before committing herself to another man.

Fay later learned that God would get her a new boyfriend, a new girlfriend, and many other new relationships as she walked in His truth, shared her faith with others, and waited for His timing and His direction.

Are you making choices, trusting people all too quickly and landing in hot water more times than you care to? The world's version of trust fails miserably most of the time because that trust is based on the wrong things. If we trust because of God's love and God's provision, because of what His word teaches, then we have some facts at our fingertips on which to base our trust in another human.

Father, Your Word has all the answers and will take me where You want me to go, whether in a new relationship or in a new direction. Help me be patient to learn what I need to learn before I make the wrong choice. AMEN.

NOTES

Let the morning bring me word of Your unfailing love, for I have put my trust in You. Show me the way I should go for to You I lift up my soul.
Psalm 143:8

Freedom to Know God's Will

Dix marveled, as she looked around the rally. Two years ago, she'd never been on a motorcycle. Now, she was part of a biker group who not only attended rallies but also helped the organizers handle security and clean up garbage, anything to make the rally a success. Remembering her transition to this state, Dix shook her head. She'd wanted to go home so badly when they'd first moved.

"I miss the family," Dix swiped at large crocodile tears of self-pity. "I want to go home." She moved toward a box, one of many that she'd still not unpacked.

Her husband Gary's sad face spoke volumes. "I accepted this transfer with your approval. We could have stayed where we were but you enthusiastically talked about our new adventure. You knew we'd be away from the kids and grandchildren, but you'd insisted you were okay with that," he reminded her. **NOTES**

"I know. I know. I didn't expect to miss everyone so much. Didn't we think you'd be the one homesick?" Dix looked toward him with pleading eyes, begging for his understanding.

Gary understood but couldn't do a thing about it. He'd burned his bridges when he'd accepted this job offer.

Dix prayed long and hard the morning they attended their new church for the first time. God told her that home was where He was. She could hardly believe the peace those comforting words brought to her soul. God reminded her of the most important thing, His unfailing love.

Dix proceeded to set out in faith and trust that they were where God wanted them to be. Her home sickness vanished the minute she walked into the church and felt the very presence of God Himself. She was home.

Since then, they'd made a point of searching to see where God wanted them. They'd joined the church but somehow God let them know that since Gary enjoyed riding a motorcycle that there was work to be done for Him in that culture. God changed Dix's heart toward bikers and moved them to the secular rally sites with His blessing.

Dix and Gary learned that as long as they trusted the Lord, God would show them the way. Do you trust God for your next move, next decision, or next step? As long as you trust in your own intellect or your own capabilities, you'll miss out on the adventure of a lifetime. You never know what God has planned for you unless you take that step of faith and follow Him out of your comfort zone.

Father God, thank you for bringing me where You are so I can walk where You want me to walk. Thank You for showing me how to serve others and giving me the opportunity to share my faith with whomever I collide with along Your path. AMEN.

Let no debt remain outstanding except the continuing debt to love one another, for he who loves his fellowman has fulfilled the law.
Romans 13:8

NOTES

Freedom to Love One Another

Years later, it seemed kind of foolish but back then the hurt was real. Benny remembered his father's distance, his contention that he loved both his sons but Benny also remembered his father's actions that spoke louder than words to the contrary.

When Benny had raced on the school varsity team, his father was nowhere to be seen. But he'd shown up for Joel's school play. When Benny had earned the role of lead in his senior drama, his father had been too busy at work to take the time off opening night but when Joel had earned a medal on the swim team, their dad was cheering for him from the bleachers.

The memories no longer had the power to hurt because Benny had resolved not to let them control his life. He'd forgiven his dad a long time ago and now had an easy relationship with the older man, one that would not have been possible if Benny hadn't made the choice to forgive.

The Bible talks about us not letting a debt remain and in this verse the debt is anger, hatred, and unforgiveness. Our only debt is to love one another. Jesus spoke of this commandment when he told his disciples that after the first command to love God with all our heart, soul, and mind, the most important one was to love our neighbors as ourselves. Our neighbors are anyone who lives on this earth with us; our brothers, sisters, fathers, mothers, and everyone else.

Are you harboring anger toward a deed long forgotten by the one you are angry with? Do you hold unforgiveness in your heart and have you discovered that the only one hurting is you? There's a reason God asks us to forgive. Most often, we are the only ones hurting when we hold a grudge and it destroys us from the inside out. Those feelings can control where

NOTES

we go, who we share our faith with, or not as the case may be, and so many other things that hurt the kingdom of God Almighty.

Entire church bodies split when unresolved anger flows through the congregation. Our example of Christian love gets blown right out the window and non-believers question why in the world they'd want what we have to offer. Love is important, not a feeling but an action. Who do you need to show love to today?

Father, I ask Your forgiveness first for being angry with_______. Give me the strength to go to this person and seek their forgiveness, not because they deserve it, but because of my love for You and Your love for me. AMEN.

He replied, "You are talking like a foolish woman. Shall we accept good from God and not trouble? In all this Job did not sin in what he said.

Job 2:10

Freedom to Hope

Jeri mechanically filled the dishwasher and turned it on. She moved toward the laundry room on wooden legs and placed another load in the dryer. The foundation of her world had cracked wide open leaving a gaping wound that she was sure would never heal. It was as if an earthquake had shattered everything she held dear.

She sat on the sofa and sobbed great tears of sorrow at the loss of innocence and the feeling of betrayal by the very God she'd chosen to follow. He was supposed to protect her family from just such a tragedy. She wanted to hide, find a mountaintop away from prying eyes, and never again talk to anyone.

Jeri was traumatized as are many people, day in and day out, who live in this fallen world.

We never know when someone or something is going to shake us out of our comfortable existence, take us for a ride down the slide of sorrow and shame. We can do all we can to prevent a child from making wrong choices but in the end it's up to them. We can seek all the medical advice available and still a husband keels over with a massive coronary.

NOTES

God's enemy, the one who would infuse himself on the throne of heaven, is also our enemy. By hurting us, his hope is to hurt the God we love. During times of trials and hurt, God is sometimes the only source of comfort. As long as we keep our eyes on Him, whatever we are going through will be bearable. It's when we focus on ourselves and how bad we feel that the problem looms large and the solution unattainable.

Job knew this. He knew that God never promised us a rose garden. In fact, His Word tells us that living as a Christian in this world is hard. He also said He'd walk with us through any trial as He did for Daniel in the fiery furnace and in the Lion's den.

Do you have a fiery furnace to walk through? Are

the lions nipping at your heels about to devour you? Turn your face toward heaven, as Job did, and watch how God will take this situation and teach you, refine you, and mold you to more clearly reflect Christ to your world than ever before.

Father, I love You. Save me from the fiery furnace but Lord, if that's not your plan, then walk through the furnace with me. Help me become more sanctified, more Christ-like through this situation. AMEN.

Be kind and compassionate to one another, forgiving each other, just as in Christ God forgave you.
Eph. 4:32

NOTES

Freedom from Jealousy

Betsy choked back the cruel remark just in time. She almost felt the color green wash over her as she listened to Ann describe another Christmas gift she'd received just that morning. Betsy knew Ann wasn't bragging, just marveling at the kindness of the people in her life.

Ann was a widow, living alone in a small two bedroom home. Her health was not so great. In fact some days, she could hardly walk. But nevertheless, whenever someone needed her to decorate a table for them, cook a meal, or supply them with cookies, Ann would do so. When her hands were hurting so bad that she thought she'd scream, she still put a casserole together to welcome a new neighbor, or a new baby into the church family. Ann knew how to be kind. She also knew how to graciously receive kindness too.

Betsy wanted to shout, "I don't want to hear about how people give you so many gifts," but she didn't. She wanted to tell Ann not to phone her anymore but she didn't do that either. Ann was the only one who phoned her on a regular basis. Ann was her friend and Betsy could not afford to lose the only friend she had.

Two lives lived in complete contrast; one woman, kind and compassionate while the other a loner, looking after her own needs and wants with never a thought for anyone else. The Bible tells us to be kind to one another, reflecting Christ to the people God brings into our lives. For Ann this was as natural as breathing. Betsy, on the other hand, hardly ever thought about what she could do for someone else.

Is there someone in your neighborhood who could use a visit? Do you know of a person who's not well and could use a card or a phone call? There are many ways we can show kindness or receive kindness. Either way, the person on the giving or the receiving end will be blessed.

Father God, please take away my selfish attitude. Make acts of kindness, random, and as easy as breathing. Give me Your Spirit of kindness as I step out for the first time to do something for someone else. Give me a new habit, Lord. AMEN.

NOTES

Your love has given mine great joy and encouragement, because you, brother, have refreshed the hearts of the saints.
Philemon 1:7

Freedom to Laugh

Dali put the finishing touches on her dinner table. “Digger, can you fill this water pitcher with ice, put some ice in these glasses, and then refill this other pitcher with ice and water, pleeeeese?” She looked at her husband with that ‘you’re the only person in the world who can do this for me’ look.

Digger laughed. He knew his wife and knew that everything had to be just so for this dinner party. “Why do you fuss so?” he asked but he already knew the answer. Their friends loved to come to her dinners and she knew that having things just right was part of the attraction. But the other part was the fun she created. No two dinner parties were alike.

“You know why. Besides, I have put a lot of trouble into this meal and I want the presentation to be as appealing as the taste of the food. These are our friends and I want them to feel as if I find them important enough for me to care about the details.” Dali

NOTES

continued to straighten this and that before beginning the finishing touches to the food. "Would you light all those candles? Everything is ready and they'll be here any minute."

Dali went in search of the game 'Catch Phrase'. They hadn't played this game with these particular friends and she wanted something fun for them to do after dinner. That's what this evening was all about...fun.

Dali and Digger had a great time when they invited friends over. Some of their meals had a theme, some were eaten just with their hands and some were elegant and formal. They laughed, kidded one another, but before the evening was over, they prayed for each other

Dali and Digger took the words in Philemon seriously. They had fun and they refreshed each other before calling it a night. Their home was one of laughter most of the time and they wanted to share some of those good memories with friends in order to make them feel special and loved.

When was the last time you invited someone over for some stimulating conversation? Do you know how to have a good time with some good clean fun? You may not have sparkling crystal to grace your table but do your friends feel welcome when they sit down and do you do the best you can to refresh them when they visit?

Father, help me refresh the people in my life when we are together. Help me find interesting ways to share Your love with them, to help them enjoy simple pleasures. AMEN.

NOTES

Another of His disciples, Andrew, Simon Peter's brother, spoke up. "Here is a boy with five small barley loaves and two small fish, but how far will they go among so many? John 6:8-9

Freedom to Hold Hands with Heaven

Gloria bowed her head. She'd never prayed before but she knew that asking the Lord into her life was important, a step she should have taken long before this. Anyhow, now she would commit her life to the one person who cared the most for her wellbeing. "Jesus, I'm sorry for the choices I've made, for going my own way. Please come into my heart and make me a new person, clean from the inside out. Oh, and Lord, if you see fit, would you take away this drug habit. Thank You."

She straightened her clothes. "I need a shower," she said to no one in particular. "I wonder if the water is hot." The pipes in the dingy apartment clanged as if in answer. Gloria walked toward the only other room and began to undress. She stepped under the warm spray and quickly washed last night's filth from her body. She'd worked the streets for three years in order to feed her habit. Every morning she vowed never again but by evening, she was hurting so badly she went out again.

The soap and water felt so good but it was already turning cold. Gloria stepped out, toweled herself off and then dressed in cleaner clothes. She had nothing that was really clean since she had to go to the Laundromat and money for that chore went into her arm. She smoothed the wrinkles out the best she could and then began to look around for something to eat.

"Hmm. I'm hungry this morning. Let's see..." Her cupboards had hardly anything in them but she managed to find a few crackers and some peanut butter. "This'll have to do." She spread a thin layer on a cracker and munched, enjoying the taste for the first time on a long time. "Lord, I guess making a commitment to you has given me some taste buds back." She chuckled.

The rest of the day, Gloria spent at work. She stocked shelves at a

NOTES

local grocery store and usually the sight of the food didn't temp her one bit but today... "Fred, can I get an advance so I can get some groceries?" She asked her manager.

"The last time I gave you an advance, you blew it and not on food. This time, you get about $25 worth of groceries and I'll take it off your paycheck." The man's kind face looked worried. He suspected that Gloria was doing drugs and prayed for her every day.

Gloria was given a second chance that day. She discovered that when you hold hands with heaven, miracles happen. She never wanted to do drugs again and her appetite for good food was just the beginning of what God would do for her. She joined a local church, at the recommendation of her boss, and later began to take some college courses to improve her work situation. Gloria was a walking miracle that inspired everyone in her neighborhood.

When we agree with God

about the things that He has placed on our heart to do, we walk as if we're in touch with heaven and others notice that about us. The small boy in the verses above did what God wanted Him to do and was able to experience the evidence of touching heaven. You too can touch heaven every day if you'll just trust God with your possessions and walk where he walks.

Father, thank you for reaching down from heaven and touching my life, Help me reach back, seek your will, and walk where you want me to walk. AMEN.

NOTES

Be still and know that I am God. I will be exalted among the nations. I will be exalted in the earth. Psalm 46:10

Freedom to Be Still

Jen sat quietly on her back deck. She listened. No television, no radio, no phone, no computer reminding her of an appointment, and no noisy air conditioner. It was so peaceful. All she could hear were the birds and an occasional squirrel scampering over her roof, or the coo of a morning dove. God's peace.

In contrast, she remembered the rally she'd just returned home from. Loud pipes roared through the campground long into the night making it close to impossible for anyone to sleep. But then the rally goers weren't there to sleep. Music blared from large speakers into the wee hours and the crowd passing by Jen's campsite was non-stop.

Jen picked up her book, a new

devotional that fed her spirit in preparation for another weekend. God's Words soothed her tired soul as she closed her eyes to talk with Him amidst the warm morning breezes. This was an oasis, this quiet time, a simple time to refresh and be still before the Lord in the quietness of His creation. Jen's heart burst with love for the One who created such a peaceful environment.

God wants us to find a balance between working for Him and sitting at His feet. Mary and Martha, two of His closest friends, were both right. We need to be working but we also need to find time to be still, to quiet our hearts and listen to what God would have us learn from Him and about Him.

Are you rushing around, hither and yon, working for the Lord in Sunday School, at Christian rallies, at secular rallies, and in a variety of other ministry events that are near your doorstep? When you come home from a rally, have you discovered that you're tired, worn out, and just plain not looking forward to the next weekend?

This is the time to spend quality time in God's presence. Let Him refresh you for the next ministry opportunity. Let Him place His thoughts and His words on your heart so that you will have something to give when the occasion arrives.

Lord, thank you for allowing me to be still in your presence. Thank you for providing a place in my home to do that and Lord, refresh me, fill me with the tools to minister when next the chance to do so comes. AMEN.

NOTES

As Jesus and His disciples were on their way, He came to a village where a woman named Martha opened her home to Him. She had a sister called Mary, who sat at the Lord's feet listening to what He said. Luke 10:38-39

Freedom to Enter the Presence of God

Georgia finished setting up her tent, inflated her air mattress, and then set the cooler of cold drinks beside her chair outside the tent. She popped the tab on a diet coke and waited. She knew she might have the chance to talk with the leader of the group and she wanted to be ready.

Georgia was part of a motorcycle gang. She cooked, cleaned, and did whatever the men asked her to do. She was not allowed to speak until spoken to and was never allowed to approach one of the men on her own. Her man had to be with her. Today, she'd caught the eye of the leader. If he was interested in her, she'd move into his tent and the rest of the gang would show her more respect. She hoped.

In contrast, God, the Almighty Creator of the Universe, allows us to sit at His feet any time we

NOTES

want to. We don't have to go through channels, wait for Him to notice us, or beg for an audience. He's there as soon as we seek Him. God created us to need His presence, to bask in His love as often as we can.

In the above verses, Jesus told Martha not to worry about the little things. He said that Mary had chosen the best thing, the most important thing and that He would not take that away from her. Mary loved the Lord, as did Martha. But Mary chose to soak in His presence, to absorb His every Word.

Do you soak up the presence of the Lord whenever you can? Do you absorb His Words so that you can minister to those around you? The Bible refers to us as God's Holy vessels. If we are empty, we have nothing to give someone else. On the other hand if all we do is study, worship, and praise, but never minister to another, our faith becomes stagnant. A vessel can only hold so much. It needs to be emptied so it can be filled again.

Dear Lord, fill me with Your presence. Prepare my heart to minister to the people You place in my path. Remind me to sit at Your feet and listen, learn and worship You on a regular basis. AMEN.

NOTES

I said, "Oh that I had the wings of a dove! I would fly away and be at rest."

Psalm 55:6

Freedom To Fly

"Some glad morning when this life is o'er, I'll fly away." Dixie sang the words silently. The tubes running down her throat made talking and singing impossible but her heart soared anyhow. It wouldn't be long now. God would let her fly through the gates of heaven and she'd see Him face to face.

"To a Home on God's celestial shore, I'll fly away." She closed her eyes. God was watching, she knew. His timing was perfect. The machines by her bedside whirred and whistled, beeped and blinked, giving her some measure of relief from the pain but it never was gone all together. Her entire family would be with her tonight and she could hardly wait. Over the last few weeks they'd taken turns being there by her bed but tonight, they'd all come at once.

"When I die, hallelujah, by and by, I'll fly away." Dixie knew that her Savior was waiting to take her home. She had that assurance and had read about His love and the home He'd prepared for her for a long time now. She'd taught her children about this home in heaven and they knew where'd she'd be as soon as she closed her eyes for the last time.

Dixie had a peace the nurses found incomprehensible. Another patient, in the next room, moaned, complained and griped about the care, or according to her, lack of care she received. She was miserable and her family didn't want to be with her at all. In fact they came as seldom as they could. That woman feared her passage into the unknown. Even though she believed death meant the end of her, she really wondered about eternity, if there was such a thing, and she was scared.

Do you long for your eternal home or are you fearful of the day when you'll breathe your last? Do you look forward to flying, to looking into the very face of God or do you fear it? Christians can know where they will be the minute after they take their last breath. They have the assurances from the Word of God.

NOTES

Lord, I have never asked you into my heart and I do fear what will become of me when I die. Please come into my heart and give me peace about Your eternal home. AMEN.

And when Daniel was lifted from the den, no wound was found on him, because he had trusted in his God.

Daniel 6:23b

Freedom Through the Fire

"Danny boy. What's this I hear about you talking to the cops?" Drake folded his huge, tattooed arms over his chest. "The boys tell me you ratted us out. That true?"

"No. I spoke to my brother-in-law, who happens to be a cop but that's all. What du ya take me for?" Danny began to pray inside. He was a new believer but his confidence in his Lord was strong. He also knew what happened to any of the gang members who talked about the club to anyone, let alone the cops.

Drake's eyes narrowed to slits. He squinted toward the man who'd informed him of Danny's duplicity. "Bear tells me you talked. You callin' him a liar."

Danny sighed. No matter what he said, he'd be in a fight, maybe to the death. "I told you. I talked to Jenna's brother but not about anything that goes on here. We're family. I have to talk to him when he visits, don't I?"

NOTES

"Let's settle this the way the Indians used to." Drake scowled. "You two fight. The one left breathing is the one who is telling the truth."

Gang members began to assemble, surrounding the two who would fight to the finish. Danny prayed all the harder. He knew he was telling the truth but Bear was named because of his size. He was a lot heftier than Danny. Bear took a swing, missed, and then scrunched up his fist for another attempt to knock his opponent off his feet. Danny side-stepped quickly and Bear swung again. Again he missed.

Two hours later, Danny was still standing, Bear was exhausted, and gang members had dissipated, bored at the outcome. Drake decided to let the matter drop until they could check out Danny's story and he ordered the fight to end. God had brought Danny through the fire, with little more than a few scratches to his neck and face.

God delivers us one of three ways when we are faced with a storm in our lives. He either delivers us from the storm, through the storm, or by the storm. If Danny had lost the fight and died, He knew that he would be in God's presence that very day. So God would have delivered him to his heavenly home by the storm he faced.

Do you face a storm in your life? Are you confident that God will deliver you? Daniel was thrown into a fiery furnace, and then into a lion's den with hungry, fearsome animals that could lick the skin right off a man. God delivered him through both those storms and he will deliver you. Just seek Him before you try to fix the mess yourself.

Father, I do want Your deliverance in my life, whatcver form that takes. I will trust that You will deliver me from, through or by the storm and that whatever means You choose will be the best for me. AMEN.

NOTES

What good is it for a man to gain the whole world, yet forfeit his soul? Or what can a man give in exchange for his soul?
Mark 8:36-37

Freedom to Believe

Samuel walked along the darkened hallway of the university. He'd made it. He had earned his BA. The four long years of struggling to understand the vast amount of knowledge his teachers pumped into his head had paid off. He couldn't wait to get home, sleep in his old bed, and begin looking for a job.

His parents raised him to believe in God. They'd taken him to church every Sunday and practiced what the preacher said. He'd left for college believing that God was real, that his parents were right, and that he'd always have that belief. Not so. He learned during the past four years that his parents were wrong. Not their fault, of course. They were just uneducated and fell under the spell of Pastor Davies.

Samuel raced towards his truck parked in a lot adjacent to his dorm room. He threw the last of his belongings into the bed of the truck and got into the driver's side. "It'll be interesting when I try to tell the folks that their beliefs are a bunch of bunk." Samuel started the engine and headed toward his home town, a few hundred miles to the east.

Samuel had gained the world's view about God and lost his soul. He would not be successful in trying to convince his parents he was right. In fact they would mourn his loss as if he'd lost his life.

Too many young people leave for school to gain a higher education. In the process they lose the only education worth attaining, their walk with God. They may have gone to church every Sunday, as Samuel did. They may even have taught in Sunday School, gone on retreat weekends with the youth group, or attended conferences where they had their faith buoyed up for the next school year. Yet, when they head off for a college whose atheistic belief system overpowers any attempt at campus ministry, they lose their faith.

Do you seek the world? Do you strive to attain a higher education and are

NOTES

you in awe of those who seem to know more than you do? The one textbook that never changes, no matter what, is the Bible itself. There's nothing wrong with more education providing you keep your priorities straight and make God #1 in your life. Don't let those who hold a skewed belief system try to tell you what to believe. Seek God's truth in the only book that holds it...the Bible.

Father God, I long to seek your truth, no matter where I go. Help me balance my time at school or at work with time for You so I can keep my perspective straight. AMEN.

Therefore since we have been justified through faith, we have peace with God through our Lord Jesus Christ. Romans 5:1

Freedom From God's Wrath

Kurt hid behind the dumpster. His nose rebelled against the overpowering odors leaking over the side of the bin. He couldn't risk getting caught, not now, not when he'd just met the woman he planned to marry one day. His thoughts bounced from remorse for the things he'd done to jubilation over his feelings for this woman. He could hear footsteps enter the passageway.

"Kurt, you in there? No use hiding. We'll find you one way or the other." The rough voice crackled with evil intent.

That voice and his heavy footsteps came closer. The monstrosity Blake called his lieutenant seemed to be on the other side of the garbage bin now. Kurt shivered. If that man caught him, it would be the end of life as he knew it.

Kurt cautiously peeked around the corner. A

piece of rust flaked off the bin and lodged itself in his eye. He blinked. Tears blurred his vision making the large man leaning on the other corner appear all the more intimidating. Kurt felt bile rise in his throat. He'd never felt this much fear before.

NOTES

"Bliss, forget him." Another man hollered down the alleyway. "His gambling debt's been paid. The boss says to let him go."

Kurt watched as Bliss turned toward the voice. "Aw, come on. Can't I hit him a little?" He pounded one massive fist into the palm of his other hand. His hands looked to Kurt as they were the same size as Kurt's head.

The distant voice appeared to shout from the street now. "Naw. Boss says to let 'im go. He may be of some use to us one day."

Bliss walked away from the dumpster. He followed the other man toward the street all the while cursing his bad luck. He seemed to really enjoy hurting people.

Kurt sighed in relief. He sank

onto the wet pavement at his feet. His knees were shaking and he felt sure he was going to be sick. "That was close," he muttered. "I wonder who paid the money." Then he began to think about the consequences of someone paying his gambling debt. "Why would they do that?"

Christ did that for us. He paid the debt we owe a just and loving God and there is no way we can ever repay Him. We deserve the anger that God has for the sin in our lives but because Christ covered our sins with His body, we are free from God's wrath. This is a free gift to us, one that we only have to accept even when we don't fully comprehend the enormity of what Christ endured.

Kurt does not know the truth about Christ yet but have you accepted this free gift? Do you know other people who need to know how much God loves them? Keep in mind that acceptance requires repentance, an admission from the heart that what we have done is wrong. We then turn away from the sinful lifestyle we engaged in and walk step by step in freedom from sin's bondage with Christ.

Father, thank You for a love so outstanding I am not able to fully understand. I accept that love gift and want nothing more than to live my life pleasing You and sharing my faith with those who still don't know about your love for them. AMEN.

NOTES

I will walk about in freedom for I have sought out your precepts.
Psalm 119:45

Freedom to Experience New Things

Dwayne rushed home from work, excitement tingling through his body as if he'd been given an infusion of the best nutrients money could buy. He couldn't wait to tell Betsy about the new motorcycle he'd just bought.

He slammed the door, anxious to share his excitement with his best friend. "Betsy, come look at this." He waved the sales receipt in the air.

"I'm coming." Her voice sounded as if it came from the back bedroom. He heard her footsteps over the sound of his boots pacing on the kitchen's tiled floor. Dwayne could not remember ever being this excited about something. He just knew Betsy would be just as happy.

Her smiling face appeared around the corner. Dwayne motioned her to sit at the table. "Hon, I bought it. The most perfect motorcycle ever. Just right for the two of us." His words were delivered with a staccato effect getting louder with each phrase. His smile covered his face.

NOTES

"For the two of us? Dwayne, I don't mind you riding a motorcycle if that's what you want, but I don't even own a pair of jeans. I think I'll pass." Betsy's resolve showed clearly on her face.

"But, I thought..."

"Dwayne, I will not ride a motorcycle. I have my women's groups and you'll have bikers. That's ok, isn't it?" Betsy looked for her husband's approval.

Dwayne's disappointment hit him like a brick. He could see his dream of the two of them in ministry together flying right out the window. "I wanted you and I to do something together. I wanted us to join that Christian Biker group and serve God as a team. Don't you see the possibility in that?"

"Dwayne, I'll pray about it but I really feel God has me where He wants me." She got up from the table dismissing Dwayne's disappointment with a belief he'd get over it. For the next two weeks, Betsy watched as one ministry group and then the other folded because they couldn't find anyone to serve on the executive. The place she'd thought God wanted her changed and little by little she began to see the need in the biker culture.

One morning, she stopped Dwayne on his way toward the garage with the keys to his beautiful blue Harley dangling from his fingers. "Do you think you could drive me to work?"

Dwayne let out a breath, surprise written all over him when he spotted the crisp new jeans she wore. He reached a shelf near the bike and pulled down a helmet, just her size. Now Betsy was the one surprised.

"How did you know I'd change my mind?" She couldn't help the smile that streaked across her face.

"I just knew God wanted us to be a team and that He would open your heart to this new adventure one day. God has many new horizons for us to explore, if only we trust Him enough to let go of the familiar and follow Him. Dwayne hugged his wife and then proceeded to show her how she should ride... be-hind him all the way.

God has a wonderful plan with adventure at every turn. Do you miss God's best for you? Do you miss the new things He wants to show you? Take time today to really listen and then follow Him wherever He leads with confidence and excitement coursing through your veins.

Father God, help me trust in You as my travel agent. Take me to the places You would have me go and open doors so I can share Your love with the people You bring before me. AMEN.

NOTES

Not only so, but we ourselves, who have the first fruits of the Spirit groan inwardly as we wait eagerly for our adoption as sons, the redemption of our bodies. For in this hope we were saved. But hope that is seen is no hope at all. Who hopes for what he already has? Romans 8:23-24 -248

Freedom for Eternity

Have you ever looked back on your life and wondered where the anxiety, worry, anger, fear, and all those other qualities are? What happened to that woman or man who was afraid to try new things, who lacked the self-confidence to stand up in front of people and give a testimony? Where did he or she go?

Sheila wondered just that. When she'd left high school, she was afraid of her own shadow. Her timidity caused her to lose the only job she'd ever wanted. When a young man paid attention to her, she was so grateful she'd do anything to keep him. Of course, as soon as he got what he wanted, she was history.

The choices she'd made back then were based on

what other people wanted her to do. God was not part of the equation. Then one day, she met Him face to face and life had not been the same since.

Marriage, kids, great friends, challenging opportunities, and adventure kept her on her toes every day, sharpened her senses, and gave her the confidence and purpose to walk where God wanted her.

God has given us an insatiable desire to be free; free from bondage to sin, free from anxiety and worry, free from physical hurt and emotional pain, so that He can satisfy this core need and we'll realize He's the only one who can. Sheila knew where her source for freedom lay. She discovered God and told anyone who wanted to know, how to be free for eternity.

Father, I love You. I long to experience the freedom only You can provide. Please release me from all the things that hold me back from truly serving You by serving others. AMEN.

NOTES

The righteous will flourish like a palm tree, they will grow like a cedar of Lebanon.

Psalm 92:12

Freedom to Live a Full Life

Cynthia checked her calendar one more time. She could hardly believe they were leaving for South Carolina already. It seemed so long ago that they'd planned this trip. She wondered how many pictures she'd take, pictures that she'd use to remind people of God's glory and His wonderful creation. She moved toward the garage, looking for her scuba gear.

Cynthia checked her tank, made sure her flippers, buoyancy compensator, and snorkel were packed and then rolled her wet suit into a ball. She tucked it into her duffle on top of the other gear. She had everything she needed to explore the depths off the coast near the beach house they'd rented for the week. Life was fun sometimes.

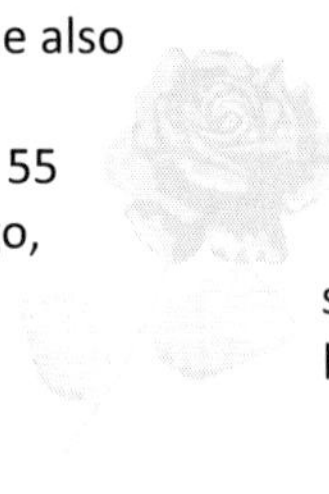

She also knew that life could be lonely. When her husband of 55 years had died three years ago, she'd thought she'd never survive. God had sustained her as He'd promised. He'd brought a new woman friend into her life, another widow. This woman loved God, life, and adventure all at the same time. They took college classes together and learned to scuba dive last spring. They prayed together and went diving together. They even went to a local pool every day to keep in shape.

NOTES

Cynthia also had three grandchildren who she loved to spend time with. They would watch her ride up on her Harley and giggle, streaking toward the sidewalk asking grandma to take them for a ride. Life with grandma, they knew, was never dull.

Life doesn't have to be dull and boring. God has given us the freedom to enjoy his creation and live a life full of adventure. He brings people from all walks of life our way, people who either encourage or discourage us but people He wants to love through us anyway.

Have you looked for your adventure today? What have you always wanted to do that you keep putting off? A movie called 'The Bucket List' is about two older men who have been given a life expectancy much shorter than they'd anticipated. Cancer runs rampant through them and they undergo treatment but soon realize it's not working. So they formulate a list, one that keeps getting longer with each new experience. This list is all the things they want to do before they kick the bucket.

Do you have a bucket list? Make one with God as your partner and see where He'll take you over the next years of your life.

Father, thank You for not expecting us to sit in a rocking chair all day once we've reach a certain age. Thank You for not using the term 'retire' in Your Book. Thank You for giving us purpose, fulfillment, and adventure, as well as confidence to learn new things throughout our life. AMEN.

About the Author

Barbara Ann Derksen has over 2500 articles published as well as three novels, a devotional, and two series of six children's books. She's a member of American Christian Fiction Writer's and Christian Writer's Fellowship International and is represented by Joyce Hart of Hartline Literary Agency.

Barbara is also a member of Christian Motorcyclists Association (CMA) along with her husband of 39 years. CMA is an evangelistic organization that goes into the highways and byways to reach lost bikers for Christ. Their goal is to change the world, one heart at a time. Barbara has a heart for the lost and has worked with organizations like Christian Women's Clubs, Successful Living, and her church to bring people into fellowship with Christ all of her Christian life. She wants the world to know her Savior and the freedom she has discovered since turning her life over to him.

In *Two Up, Riding With The Lord*, Barbara Ann Derksen creatively illustrates the importance of what it means to be God's adopted child… **Accepted**, **Secure**, **Significant**, and **Free**… through faith in God's one and only Son, the Lord Jesus Christ. You will discover the privileges of being a child of God, your strength as a believer, and the power given to you by God's Holy Spirit as you spent time in His Word through these daily readings.